A Peaceable Economy

Visions and Voices
Personal Perspectives on Justice and Peace

Life itself is endangered today, yet Christians around the world have vital insights, convictions, and traditions to engage positively in fostering life, confronting cultures and practices of death, and building justice and peace.

Exploring many of the issues raised by the theme, "God of Life, lead us to justice and peace," this series offers brief volumes from leading Christian thinkers and activists. Centered on the four arenas of Just Peace (peoples, community, marketplace, and the earth), the books present strong opinions forcefully argued on many of the most pressing and important issues of our day. Initial volumes include:

Clare Amos
Peace-ing Together Jerusalem

Edward Dommen
A Peaceable Economy

Jessie Fubara-Manuel
Giver of Life, Hear Our Cries for Justice

Tatha Wiley
Misusing Sin

Donald Miller
From Just War to Just Peace

A Peaceable Economy

Edward Dommen

**World Council
of Churches**
Publications

THE PEACEABLE ECONOMY

WCC Publications is the book publishing programme of the World Council of Churches. Founded in 1948, the WCC promotes Christian unity in faith, witness and service for a just and peaceful world. A global fellowship, the WCC brings together more than 349 Protestant, Orthodox, Anglican and other churches representing more than 560 million Christians in 110 countries and works cooperatively with the Roman Catholic Church.

Opinions expressed in WCC Publications are those of the authors.

Scripture quotations are from the New Revised Standard Version Bible, © copyright 1989 by the Division of Christian Education of the National Council of the Churches of Christ in the USA. Used by permission.

Cover design: Julie Kauffman Design
Cover image: *The Peaceable Kingdom*, Edward Hicks (1780–1849)
Interior design and typesetting: 4 Seasons Book Design/Michelle Cook
ISBN: 978-2-8254-1639-6

World Council of Churches
150 route de Ferney, P.O. Box 2100
1211 Geneva 2, Switzerland

http://publications.oikoumene.org

Contents

Preface

> May we look upon our treasures, the furniture of our
> houses and our garments, and try whether the seeds
> of war have nourishment in these our possessions.
> – John Woolman (1720–1772), *A Plea for the Poor*

This is a book about human nature. Economic theory has a fairly all-embracing view of what makes people tick. Theorists of war also have a view of human nature. The two views are similar in many ways, which is hardly surprising since both are concerned with the behaviour of the same people. They part company when it comes to social dynamics. War theorists are acutely aware of processes that feed on themselves, whereas orthodox economists prefer to see the economy as a system in, or at least seeking to reach, a stable equilibrium. However, other observers of the economy, including authors of the Bible in particular but also some present-day academics, join the war theorists in attaching great importance to cumulative social processes.

Economists generally consider their discipline to be a science. They therefore tend to expound their views with the unyielding conviction of those who are convinced they possess the truth. Theorists of war, on the other hand, consider their discipline to be an art. Thus, paradoxically, they can be more pragmatic and flexible in their approach to social reality.

Part One of this book explores the theory and practice of economics and its similarities to war. Part Two envisions an alternative, a peaceable economy, and inquires into its conditions. It starts by describing several ideal or utopian economies. Like the stable equilibrium of the orthodox economy, utopias are supposed to be an ultimate resting place. Once it is reached, there is no call to move on. The book then proceeds to ask whether ideal economies of such a kind can actually be reached from here. It depends on the nature of the people who would inhabit it. Ideal economies require ideal inhabitants. Human behaviour would have to change.

Churches have made it their job over the centuries to teach people how to behave better and to encourage them to change their ways. This kind of activity is prescriptive, not descriptive. Oddly enough, economists, although they claim to be scientists, are no less prescriptive, striving to bring people's behaviour into line with the requirements of their models. Economists have more in common with theologians than many would like to admit.

In any event, history gives little evidence that the efforts of conscious or unconscious moralists have actually achieved much in the way of moral progress. That, however, justifies neither escapism nor defeatism. All we can do is try.

Part One

Economies and Violence
Related forms of social interaction

1. Economies and Economics

Economies are the aspects of society that concern the organization of livelihood.[1] A variety of economies have existed in different periods and places; indeed different forms of economy can exist within one society at the same time with more or less intimate relations between them.

Today's globalized economy exhibits a definite pecking order between forms of economic organization. There is a dominant form, simply called "the Economy" and a range of lesser ones that bear names qualified by adjectives: alternative, subsistence, traditional (whatever that means), indigenous, collective, etc. Serious economists may glance briefly at them with degrees of amusement, if not condescension, when they do not abandon the study of them to anthropologists and such. Political correctness may incite the Economy to treat them politely in appropriate circumstances—provided these inferior forms do not stand in the way of their hegemony. Should they do so, they become heresy, to be persecuted and if possible eradicated like heresies in any major religion.

The Study of Economics

Economics, the academic study of economies, is therefore the defence of orthodoxy, not an encyclopedic enquiry into all existing economies, not to mention all conceivable ones. It is thus very different from biology or botany. It is more akin to theology as taught in a confessional training institution, a seminary for instance, or to politics as taught in a party training college.

Throughout a large part of the 20th century, two forms of economic organization competed for world hegemony; and for part of that period a third form, fascism, also played a significant role. All of them had their apologists, their analyses, and their academic centres. No one of them could ignore the other two, which imposed a degree of comparative thinking if not open-mindedness on all of them. On the other hand, they could all crush, subdue, or at best ignore the other lesser forms of economy to be found in the world. In a similar way, the main Christian denominations reached agreements to share the Pacific island communities among themselves, not fighting each other but recognizing their shared objective of supplanting the local religions.

Some definitions for a start

Let us start with two "inside" definitions of the discipline. In examining them we must however remember that the discipline concerns itself with only a limited range of forms of economic organization and that the insiders who formulated the definitions regard their activity as a science. Many readers of this book will be able to ask themselves whether theology is a science in the same way.

Two definitions are helpful. The first comes from Wikipedia: "Economics is the social science that analyses the production, distribution, and consumption of goods and services;[2] and the second from Lionel Robbins: "Economics is the science which studies human behaviour as a relationship between ends and scarce means which have alternative uses."[3]

In exploring some of the detailed implications of these definitions, we shall in fact be taking a few examples to confront the self-perception of the discipline of economics with the realities of the Economy, and occasionally of other forms of economy too. The first definition, like many others, focuses on goods and services. Some others include 'exchange', while a few recognize that disposal is also involved. The list of functions can indeed be expanded or contracted.

Goods & services

Traditionally in economics, goods are physical objects and services are immaterial. At times in the history of economic thought, the distinction has given rise to extensive debate. It can be argued that the use value of a good, as opposed to its exchange value, depends on the flow of services it provides. Let us treat the debate as metaphysical and ignore the distinction. To stress the intimacy of the couple, we shall systematically use an "&" to link the two.

Goods & services consist of anything that people would like to have i) to hold, keep, show off or store away; ii) to consume; iii) to use to acquire something else they would rather have, either through exchange or as intermediate goods, inputs into a process producing something wanted more directly for use.

Goods and bads

We all know that good and evil are inextricably entangled. "So I find it to be a law that when I want to do what is good, evil lies close at hand" (Rom. 7:21). The goods and bads that compose the economy are entangled in the same way. If goods & services are good at all, they must be of benefit to at least some people. One can imagine cases in which they may be good for everyone, but these are extremely rare. In other cases, they may benefit some and harm no one; they are rare too. Generally, one person's meat is another's poison: the production, distribution, consumption, or disposal of something to the benefit of some generates externalities (that is, other effects) to the detriment of others. The opposite can also occur: something that benefits some may benefit others as a side-effect. People who plant colourful flowers on their balcony railing give pleasure not only to themselves but to passers-by as well. Externalities can be negative or positive; both can indeed occur at once.

The services that economies produce include elements like power or prestige, and by the same token their converse, humiliation or powerlessness, as well as the means of transmission from the one to the other, like oppression or envy. The seven deadly sins can all be generated within the economy and can therefore often be regarded as products of the economy: wrath, greed, sloth, pride, envy, gluttony, and lust (especially if it is taken in its broad sense of a passionate desire, whatever it may be for). Ambition, another driver of economic activity, is one of the generators of several of the seven sins. Hierarchies and pecking orders are as intrinsic to businesses as they are to armies. Definitions of 'money' often include a specific reference to power, specifically the power to acquire whatever is for sale. Since in many types of economy the range of goods & services available in exchange for money is wide, money is considered to provide a general command over things and people. Some would even say that it is a yardstick of power.

Among goods & services, public goods and services have the defining characteristics of being non-rival and non-exclusive: one person's using them in no way prevents anyone else from using them at the same time, and if they are available to anyone they are automatically available to everyone within the relevant area: a street light, for instance. Some economists prefer the term 'common goods', associating the concept with that of the commons.[4] For readers with theological leanings, however, there is a danger of confusing that term with 'the common good', a useful but different concept central to Catholic social teaching.

Within the community concerned, public goods have the virtue of being immune to the rivalry, envy, and greed that drive the conflictual tendencies in the economy. On the other hand, exceptions like the atmosphere apart, they are not available beyond a particular area. This may be the inevitable consequence of their intrinsic characteristics (the light of a street light only carries so far), but the temptation exists to determine and police the boundaries so as to restrict the range of beneficiaries. Defending boundaries is one of the most traditional types of war.

Nature and nurture

Not all goods & services are produced in the sense of being the result of human decisions. The sun's rays are more than a mere example: they constitute an essential source of energy that serves to counterbalance the energy lost through entropy.[5] However, the gifts of nature generally require human intervention to put them in a form that people can exploit. Furthermore, whatever may be considered a gift of nature is usually tucked away among human constructs. To try and extricate them is a finicky job and of little practical use. The issue recalls the nature/nurture debate with respect to human character, although here it stretches from the human personality to all aspects of creation. For present purposes we may leave it aside.

Exchange

Several versions of the first definition of economics, especially in the US, add the word "exchange," thus implicitly excluding from the remit of economics any form of distribution that does not involve exchange. Apart from excluding centrally planned economies, it ignores production for own consumption. Subsistence production is important, if not essential, to the livelihood or quality of life of a large proportion of humanity. Adding "exchange" to the definition also excludes goods that are so abundant and widespread that there is no call to engage in any social activity to enjoy them.

Insisting on exchange as a criterion excludes gifts and other unrequited transfers, yet these are essential to the economy as a network of social relationships. Indeed gifts can be an important source of friendly relations in the peaceable economy. Marcel Mauss (1923–1924) emphasized the relationships established through a sequence of gifts given and gifts made in return as a form of exchange spread over time. This reassures economists obsessed with exchange as a defining characteristic of the object of their study and helps explain Mauss's popularity among economists. As he himself recognized, such networks can create burdens of obligation that are far from fostering friendly relations. The type of exchange Mauss described undoubtedly exists, but so do unrequited gifts.

Conversely, to insist on exchange as an essential characteristic of economies ignores two forms of behaviour that are especially relevant to peaceable economies because they are so essentially unpeaceable: expropriation and imposition. Appropriating other people's possessions for one's own benefit is an everyday occurrence in the world economy. From mining concessions to the facilities for mega sporting events like the Olympic Games, from large hydroelectric dams to large-scale land grabs, powerful economic interests seize other people's land, housing, or livelihoods and disrupt their cultures. Conversely, powerful economic interests impose burdens on weaker communities, for instance by taking their water without compensation or dumping toxic waste on them.

Disposal[6]

The first definition of economics hardly ever includes 'disposal' in the list of activities that make up an economy. Yet it is an integral part of the life cycle of goods & services. The wanted and the unwanted outputs of the economy are inextricably entangled with each other, rather like good and evil.

Industrial ecology strives systematically to put the refuse back into the economic cycle, to turn it from waste into a resource again. Such recycling existed long before industry: it is a normal characteristic of traditional agriculture. It is a peaceable approach, akin to the advice attributed to Abraham Lincoln: "The best way to destroy an enemy is to make him a friend."

Unfortunately, such a desirable outcome is all too rarely achieved in either case. Unwanted outputs are produced during production processes, like greenhouse gases or nuclear waste in the production of energy, or tailings and poisoned water in mining. Final products that are no longer wanted or serviceable also need to be disposed of.

Since by definition no one wants this refuse, it can only be inflicted on unwilling takers. Buyers and sellers have a shared interest in leaguing together to impose the costs of disposal on third parties. These are obviously weaker than the others, otherwise they would refuse the burden. This part of the economic cycle is patently warlike, with victors who have the power to get rid of their refuse on the losers. Victory is all the easier if the vanquished are unaware of what is going on. Hence the discretion of the uranium mining industry about the damage it inflicts on the health of its workers, or the dumping of toxic waste in places like Haiti, where the people were even persuaded that it was fertilizer and thus encouraged to spread it about.[7] When waste disposal results in damage to health and the resource base, or in impoverishment, or more fundamentally expresses contempt or disregard for others, it generates frustration and resentment; it nourishes the seeds of war.

On the other hand, waste disposal is a form of economic activity providing employment and income to many. Not only to powerful public authorities, large enterprises, or mafia-type organizations who simply get rid of it, but also to those who play their part in industrial ecology by collecting scrap metal or empty bottles, not forgetting the countless people who, for lack of a better choice, live on rubbish dumps as scavengers.

In any event, the definition of economics is incomplete without "disposal." Let us therefore complete the first definition as follows: "Economics analyses the production, distribution, consumption, and disposal of goods and services." One could even specify "Economics analyses *the cycle of* production, distribution, consumption, and disposal of goods & services," for indeed whatever is thrown away is likely to reappear somewhere in the cycle later on, as a desired input or as a nuisance that has to be dealt with in the further functioning of the cycle, or as both at once. Thus, kitchen waste can be turned into compost to feed the next generation of vegetables. Nuclear waste has to be managed for thousands of years. It imposes a burden of work on future generations until they invent some way of using it.[8]

The economy is a cycle, but it is not a closed one. On the one hand, it is constantly receiving fresh supplies, especially of energy from the sun. On the other hand, any resource once used degrades into greater disorder through the dissipation of energy within the system according to the law of entropy; it can be recycled only at increasing ecological cost at each round.[9]

Scarcity

According to the second definition, economics is essentially conflictual. There is not enough to go around, at least of the goods with which the economy is concerned, so economic agents must compete for their share of them. This definition was contested from the moment Lionel Robbins formulated it—for a reason not of scarcity but of overabundance, but which still sprang from a concern for social peace. No one would contest that employment is an economic issue. In the mass unemployment of Europe in the 1930s, the dominant economic problem was not that society had to choose between alternative uses for scarce labour, but that there was no use at all for a significant part of it. The economy did not want all the labour on offer, preferring to leave it unused. Families were not only left with no source of income, the economy simply rejected them, treating them as worthless in all senses of the word. This form of scorn for people was among the main causes of the second world war.

Unemployment is still today a bane of the economies of most rich countries, running at more than 10 percent in most of the EU, and over 25 percent in some of its member countries. In other words, more than one person in four in the latter countries who would like to work and is in the socially acceptable age group cannot find work. They are unwanted, surplus to requirements.

Reformation theologian John Calvin insists: "We know that for artisans and workers their income lies in their being able to earn a living; they do not have their monies invested in meadows and fields. As God has placed their life in their hands, i.e. in the work they do, if they are deprived of the necessary means, it is just as if their throats had been cut."[10] Causing the death of people is the hallmark of war, but the incidence of death also provides an effective tool for analyzing how an economy functions.

In Europe and North America today, many of those who have the resources to provide workers with the means to work prefer to do something else with their capital. It has alternative uses, but that does not mean that it is scarce; on the contrary, the sums washing about on the world's financial markets grow by feeding on themselves. The preferred uses may be utterly futile;[11] that is indeed the nub of the debate about whether one can distinguish the financial from the real economy. Finance serves the real economy only in so far as it funds investment in real capital that provides jobs for people wanting to work and goods & services for the common good. Calvin again: "The air must resound with shouts ... against those who have not put to use the means which have been committed to their care."[12] To withhold capital from this service is also warlike behaviour, similar to a siege or a blockade.

Economics is sometimes called "the dismal science." The nickname is generally seen as inspired by the views of the British Anglican clergyman Thomas Robert Malthus (1766–1834).[13] He argued that while population tended to grow by geometrical progression (1-2-4-8-etc.), subsistence grew only by arithmetical progression (1-2-3-4-etc.). "The ultimate check to population appears then to be a want of food, arising necessarily from the different ratios according to which population and food increase."[14] Apart from "preventive checks" (broadly speaking, family planning), the "positive checks" that keep population in line with subsistence "include every cause, whether arising from vice or misery, which in any degree contributes to shorten the natural duration of human life. Under this head, therefore, may be enumerated all unwholesome occupations, severe labour and exposure to the seasons, extreme poverty, bad nursing of children, great towns, excesses of all kinds, the whole train of common diseases and epidemics, wars, plague and famine."[15]

We find here an early presentation of structural violence, to which we shall return. Note that Malthus includes war among the normal regulatory mechanisms of the economy. Above all, for the inventor of the dismal science, scarcity not only exists, it prevails. It defines the framework within which the whole economy functions.

The ideas of Jean-Jacques Rousseau (1712–1778) were part of Malthus' intellectual environment. Along the same lines as Malthus, he saw the golden age as ending when the number of humans had expanded to the point where there was no space to spare and the age of scarcity dawned.

> [W]hen inheritances so increased in number and extent as to occupy the whole of the land, and to border on one another, one man [sic] could aggrandise himself only at the expense of another; at the same time the supernumeraries ... were obliged to receive their subsistence, or steal it, from the rich; and this soon bred, according to their different characters, dominion and slavery, or violence and rapine. The wealthy, on their part, had no sooner begun to taste the pleasure of command, than they disdained all others, and, using their old slaves to acquire new, thought of nothing but subduing and enslaving their neighbours; like ravenous wolves.[16]

Thus for Rousseau war appeared at the same time as scarcity. However, it was not scarcity itself that provoked war and disorder, but the spirit of appropriation and exclusion:

> The first man who, having enclosed a piece of ground, bethought himself of saying *This is mine*, and found people simple enough to believe him, was the real founder of

civil society. From how many crimes, wars and murders, from how many horrors and misfortunes might not any one have saved mankind, by pulling up the stakes, or filling up the ditch, and crying to his fellows, "Beware of listening to this impostor; you are undone if you once forget that the fruits of the earth belong to us all, and the earth itself to nobody.[17]

To sum up so far, for Malthus scarcity has war among its normal consequences, while for Rousseau war and scarcity go hand in hand, but both agreed that population growth had reached the point where scarcity is an inescapable fact of life.

Karl Marx's concept of the reserve army of the unemployed, which makes no secret of drawing on Malthusianism, fits into Rousseau's vision of the golden age collapsing with the private appropriation of wealth. "Big industry constantly requires a reserve army of unemployed workers … The main purpose of the bourgeois in relation to the worker is, of course, to have the commodity labour as cheaply as possible, which is only possible when the supply of this commodity is as large as possible in relation to the demand for it."[18] In other words, those who possess the other factors of production withhold them as an aggressive tactic to force into subservience those who are fortunate enough to be given work.

Mao Zedong's Great Leap Forward (1958–1961) applied this approach in an even more radical way, starving the peasants, who were the backbone of the economy, to free resources in order to create capital for a new form of economy. Between 18 and 45 million deaths are attributed to this policy.[19] War-like oppression of the weak is not confined to liberal market economies.

Sufficiency

Calvin on the other hand insists that God provides not only enough for everyone, but plenty: "God not only provides for people's necessity, and bestows upon them as much as is sufficient for the ordinary purposes of life, but ... in his goodness he deals still more bountifully with them by cheering their hearts with wine and oil. For nature would certainly be satisfied with water to drink."[20]

Mohandas K. Gandhi is often cited as saying the same thing more pithily: "Earth provides enough to satisfy every one's need, but not every one's greed." The phrase seems to be apocryphal. The website of Mani Bhavan, a Gandhi memorial centre in Mumbai, offers the following more detailed quotation as more exact:

> I suggest that we are thieves in a way. If I take anything that I do not need for my own immediate use and keep it I thieve it from somebody else. I venture to suggest that it is the fundamental law of Nature, without exception, that Nature produces enough for our wants from day to day, and if only everybody took enough for himself

and nothing more, there would be no pauperism in this world, there would be no more dying of starvation in this world. But so long as we have got this inequality, so long we are thieving.[21]

Emulation

Everyone models their consumption standards—and indeed other standards—on those of other people whom they take consciously or unconsciously as role models. It is one of the ways social cohesion and identity are constructed.

Suppose A takes B as a model. A and B may be individuals or social entities - families, or religious, ethnic or cultural communities, or companies. Status and style are not confined to consumption; they are also reflected in manners of production. Recourse to company cars or aircraft or an extravagant use of public space and precious marble in corporate offices, or on the other hand the fairness of labour relations and concern for the welfare of workers, suppliers, customers, or the surrounding community, are all forms of behaviour that can inspire emulation by other firms.

Status and style are also expressed in the ways power—political, economic, or other—is displayed and exercised. Consider how French heads of state like to be seen in gilded rooms and how the leaders of North Korea show themselves soberly dressed while the military officers around them are dripping with brass and medals.

Suppose now that *A* is striving to achieve *B's* standard, to "keep up with the Joneses." In so far as *B's* standard is more costly, this imitation already increases the scarcity of the norm-setting goods.

However, if *B* sees their status as depending on the distance between themselves and *A,* the situation becomes inextricable. When *A* succeeds in approaching *B*, *B* must flee into greater display in order to preserve self-image. There is no finishing line. In the corporate world, a few decades ago status involved market share. *A* could by definition increase its share only at the expense of its competitors, whose status thereby declined. If *B* is in a position of power, another solution is for it to deny *A* the right to imitate its style. Sumptuary rules that limit consumption of certain goods to certain classes have often been widespread. The scarcity is imposed not by objective availability but by conventional rule. Scarcity is particularly acute when *A* wants, not something like *B's,* but the very same object. An army officer wants to be dictator in the place of the current dictator. A manager wants to be boss in the place of the boss. A burglar inside a house wants the occupier's belongings. Turf wars between gangs are rivalries of this type. Conflicting territorial claims between states are an especially traditional form of it, traditionally expressing itself in war.

Unlimited wants

The website Investopedia takes the second definition of economics at the start of this chapter a small but crucial step further: "[Economics is a] social science that studies how individuals, governments, firms and nations make choices on allocating scarce resources to satisfy their unlimited wants."[22] The conflict becomes utterly inextricable if the agents' wants are unlimited: in such a situation there is no prospect of ever producing enough to overcome scarcity.

Economic growth is a present-day fetish. It rests on the assumption of unlimited wants an object of devotion in their own right rather than a means to another goal. The idol representing economic growth is GDP, Gross Domestic Product. This is a compilation of figures that compose the National Accounts, a codified set of economic statistics. The System of National Accounts (SNA)—produced under the auspices of the United Nations, the European Commission, the Organization for Economic Co-operation and Development, the International Monetary Fund, and the World Bank Group— is the internationally agreed standard set of recommendations on how to compile them.[23] National accounts were originally designed during the Great Depression of the 1920s and 1930s as tool for Keynesian management of the economy, initially to manage the creation of jobs for the unemployed (a matter of bringing surplus resources into use) and soon after to manage a war economy in which scarce resources are concentrated as effectively as possible on the war effort.

It was only much later that GDP, one of the many aggregates that can be derived from the national accounts, acquired its iconic status as a symbol of economic size, success, and even welfare. The overblown and dubious virtues of this figure are now increasingly being called into question. The Stiglitz Sen Fitoussi Report, commissioned by the French government in 2008, nicely sums up the state of the debate.[24]

It is reported that the Swiss writer Max Frisch (1911–1991) asked, "Dinosaurs survived 250 million years. How do you imagine economic growth over 250 million years?" The idea is obviously absurd. Such a span of economic growth can only run smack into the wall of scarcity. More important still for our purposes, growth of GDP ignores the fact that people pick satisfaction, pleasure, and conviviality in activities outside the economy. The Stiglitz Sen Fitoussi Report explores a number of indicators that are less inhuman and aggressive.

Is Economics a Science? Models of Reality

The definitions we have given so far generally treat economics as a science, notwithstanding the Soviet joke that if economics were a science, it would have been tested on animals first. However, although the 1995 edition of the *Concise Oxford Dictionary* defined economics as "a science," its 2001 edition shifted this to "a branch of knowledge." As one expects of a good dictionary, it is following changing usages and attitudes.

A growing school of thought among economists contests the status of the discipline as a science.[25]

What then is a science? Or more precisely, what is the use of science? Science strives to explain systematically and methodically how the world works. Its purpose is to help people find their way through the luxuriant undergrowth of reality without tripping up.

Science is undoubtedly a quest for truth, but then in turn, what is truth?[26] Firstly, truth must not only be correct, but helpful. Several truths may all explain a single situation correctly, but some may be more helpful than others depending on one's needs in a particular situation, as illustrated in the accompanying box.

How long is a metre?

The standard measure of length is the metre, a unit at a pleasantly human scale. It roughly corresponds to the length of an adult arm, or the girth of a well-fed man. It is about as long as three human feet. John Wilkins, Anglican bishop of Chester, defined it in the 17th century as the 10 millionth part of the quarter of the circumference of the Earth. The French Academy of Sciences rendered this definition official in 1791. (This lovely round number comforts those who are convinced that God designed the universe for the convenience of humanity, but I have no grounds for claiming that Wilkins, or for that matter anyone else, ever explicitly defended that view.)

Shortly after Wilkins, the Italian scientist Tito Livio Burattini defined the metre as the length of a pendulum for which the period of half a swing equals one second. Burattini's definition was sidelined because the trip through a unit of time to measure a length seemed intuitively awkward. The trouble with both these definitions is that the length varies—a tiny bit—according to geographical location. To escape from all these approximations, the metre was officially defined from 1889 to 1960 as the length between two points on a platinum-iridium rod kept in the observatory at Sèvres in France. The trouble with that definition was that the conservators were so worried about the risk of altering the length of the rod that virtually no one could get access to it.

Since 1983, the official definition of the metre is the distance travelled by light in a vacuum in $1/299\ 792\ 458$ of a second. If Burattini's definition was regarded as counter-intuitive and therefore unhelpful, what is a breathing consumer with a watch who wants to buy a length of cloth to make of the current definition? It was of course not chosen with such ordinary people in mind, but to meet the insatiable demand of scientists for precision. People buying cloth are content with notches on the counter.

Secondly, all scientific truths are provisional. They are hypotheses, regarded as true until they are proven false, and the scientist's job consists of constantly challenging them by trying to show them up as false.[27] If falsified, they are replaced by a new hypothesis that explains reality more realistically. There is something warlike in the nature of science: the defenders of the status quo, the scientific conservatives, are retrenched in their citadel, ready to repel the scientific innovators seeking to storm it.

Science is essentially curious. It is actively on the lookout for new information that may trouble its certainties. Botanists go out to search for new plants. They attempt to fit them into existing classifications while accepting that the new discovery may oblige them to revise them. Economists on the other hand tend to lack curiosity. They show little interest in unusual ways of organizing livelihood. Instead of studying them objectively, they attempt to belittle their qualities and to hector them into behaving properly. They are more like missionaries than scientists.

Science, we have said, attempts to explain reality systematically. Each truth, each fact, fits into a coherent whole held together by the rules of its logic. To falsify any element of the system weakens the overall structure, which has to be adjusted accordingly. As successive occasional adjustments add to a forest of makeshift supports, it becomes more and more difficult to move around inside the model. Or alternatively, the elegance of the original structure is maintained at the cost of becoming a work of art, perhaps beautiful to behold but with little resemblance to the realities of everyday life. At some point it becomes more convenient to abandon the old model and adopt another.

Easier said than done. Scientists who invest time, energy, and reputation in building and burnishing a model develop an affection for it. It pains them to turn their back on it. Or, to put it in more brutally economic terms, having built their castle in the air, they want to collect the rent from it.

Economists use models to present their understanding of an economic mechanism in a systematic way. The models are often presented in mathematical form. In many cases, mathematics are to economic models what a suit is to a businessperson: it is a way of dressing up to mark the distinguished status of the role one is playing. Two thousand five hundred years ago and more, the Bible presented a shrewd and coherent model of the economy in the vernacular, without hesitating to draw on pithy sayings from the popular wisdom of its time. The model is still applicable today. As recently as the mid-20th century, James Meade wrote *The Balance of Payments*, which largely contributed to his 1977 Nobel Prize in Economics, by and large in plain English. The mathematics underlying the argument was confined to a supplement in a separate volume.[28] Science need not be abstruse.

Since all models by their very nature simplify reality in order to explain it, no model can provide a complete and perfect description of the real world, even less so if it needs to be convenient as well. There can be legitimate argument about which model provides the most effective tool for dealing with the problem at hand.

In any event, one can generally trust the model-builders to have built a model that is internally consistent, so that the assumptions lead by the force of logic to the conclusions. The validity of the model can therefore be tested by confining one's efforts to examining its assumptions.

One can also check the realism of the conclusions. If they do not correspond to reality, several types of reason can be adduced. Lack of realism in the assumptions is one, but inappropriate simplification may be another: maybe the model has ignored some variables that play a significant role in the workings of the real system in all its complexity.

Most economic models claim to describe aspects of reality. On the other hand, many of them are prescriptive rather than descriptive: they present a picture of a desirable economy rather than an existing one. Having described the desirable state of affairs, it is possible to work back through the model to ascertain its assumptions, the conditions in which it could be achieved. One can then explore the realism of the assumptions, or the possibility of modifying reality so that it corresponds to the required conditions. We shall do something along these lines in Part Two.

Economic science is dominated by Anglo-Saxon thinking and cultural presuppositions. Nonetheless, many economists ignore one of the founding distinctions in Anglo-Saxon moral philosophy, the 18th-century Scottish philosopher David Hume's dictum that "is" should not be confused with "ought."[29] In economics, several prescriptive models masquerade as descriptive ones.

Let us end this enquiry into what an economy is with a third definition, subtler and more evocative than most of the ones we have explored so far. It is by Alfred Marshall (1842–1924), one of the founders of economics as an undergraduate discipline, whose *Principles of Economics* can be considered a pioneer university textbook on the subject. Setia's definition in the opening sentence of this chapter stops at the semicolon; Marshall's spells it out in more detail: "Economics is a study of mankind in the ordinary business of life; it examines that part of individual and social action which is most closely connected with the attainment and the use of the material requisites of wellbeing. Thus it is on the one side a study of wealth; and on the other, and more important side, a part of the study of man."[30]

2. Cumulative Causation
A Dynamic Common to Violence and the Economy

Take a circle, caress it and it will turn vicious.
– Eugene Ionesco, *The Bald Soprano*, 1950

Conflict and economics both partake of the same dynamic: once things start moving in a particular direction, they tend to gather momentum. The dynamic is not confined to social relations; it also determines natural processes. Hence the valleys, gorges, or canyons through which rivers run: flowing water left to itself digs itself a channel, then digs it deeper and deeper. A muscle unused will atrophy, while one that is used will grow stronger.

Mainstream economics, on the other hand, takes stable equilibrium as its ideal state. Stable equilibrium is also often found in nature, for instance in a set of marbles in a bowl. If the marbles are disturbed, they will rearrange themselves until they rest in a stable position again; it will look very much like the original position. On the other hand, Gunnar Myrdal, an unconventional economist even if he was awarded the Nobel Prize in economics in 1975, built his analysis on cumulative causation:

> My starting point is the assertion that the notion of stable equilibrium is normally a false analogy to choose when constructing a theory to explain the changes in a social system … Behind this idea is another and still more basic assumption, namely that a change will regularly call forth a reaction in the system in the form of changes which on the whole go in the opposite direction to the first change.
>
> The idea I want to expound … is that, on the contrary, in the normal case there is no such tendency towards automatic self-stabilisation in the social system. The system is by itself not moving towards any sort of balance between forces, but is constantly on the move away from such a situation. In the normal case a change does not call forth countervailing changes but, instead, supporting changes, which move the system in the same direction as the first change but much further. Because of such circular causation a social process tends to become cumulative and often to gather speed at an accelerating rate.[1]

In this passage, Myrdal stresses that he is comparing visions of Platonic ideals. He is choosing between assertions on the basis of which to build a theoretical model of social interaction. They are axioms; they are not to be established as true, but taken for granted as a starting point. To be useful, the operational criterion on which to base one's choice of axiom should be that of realism: the choice of axiom is justified by whether the model built on it reflects the way society actually works. The proof of the pudding is in the eating.

The Bible generally makes the same choice as Myrdal, taking the view that society is largely driven by cumulative processes. The vision of today's mainstream economists is less realistic. They describe or forecast actual events less well than the biblical vision of reality.

Conflict

Genesis 4 describes a spiral of violence and revenge that was current at the time, and indeed is still widespread today: "Then the Lord said to him, 'Whoever kills Cain will suffer a sevenfold vengeance" (Gen. 4:15), and later, "Lamech said to his wives . . . I have killed a man for wounding me, a young man for striking me. If Cain is avenged sevenfold, truly Lamech seventy-sevenfold" (Gen. 4:23-24). If Cain or Lamech deserve death for having killed, they can only be killed once in their turn. The seven or seventy-seven times thus involves killing yet more people. In societies driven by the vendetta spirit, these are generally kinsfolk of the murderer. Each new death calls up the urge for further multiplied revenge. So the process spreads from bad to worse.

In order to restrain this kind of cumulative cycle of vengeance, Exodus laid down the law limiting retaliation, reflecting a provision that the Babylonian Code of Hammurabi had established earlier: "Eye for eye, tooth for tooth, hand for hand, foot for foot, burn for burn, wound for wound, stripe for stripe" (Ex. 21:24-25). However, if that law is respected, the cycle of vengeance can still go on forever. At least it does not grow at each round, but it does ever-extending damage: "An eye for an eye makes the whole world blind."[2] The two senses of the saying deserve to be fully spelled out: apart from its direct meaning, it has the deeper one that a community that practises the law of the talion is blind to where it leads— that is, to the destruction of society.

The New Testament tackles the mechanism of cumulative causation head on. The antidote consists in putting the machine into reverse so that the cumulative process now runs in the right direction, towards peace. This is reflected at its clearest in Matthew 5:38-47:

> "You have heard that it was said, 'An eye for an eye and a tooth for a tooth.' But I say to you, Do not resist[3] an evildoer. But if anyone strikes you on the right cheek, turn the other also; and if anyone wants to sue you and take your coat, give your cloak as well; and if anyone forces you to go one mile, go also the second mile. Give to everyone who begs from you, and do not refuse anyone who wants to borrow from you.[4]

"You have heard that it was said, 'You shall love your neighbor and hate your enemy.' But I say to you, Love your enemies and pray for those who persecute you . . . For if you love those who love you, what reward do you have? Do not even the tax collectors do the same? And if you greet only your brothers and sisters, what more are you doing than others? Do not even the Gentiles do the same?

Hints of this approach can already be found in the Old Testament, at least in one of the books of wisdom: "Do not say, 'I will do to others as they have done to me; I will pay them back for what they have done'" (Prov. 24:29).

The Economy

For to those who have, more will be given, and they will have more than enough; but from those who have nothing, even what they have will be taken away. (Matt. 13:12).

This dictum pithily and accurately captures the way the economy actually works; not just today's market economy, but all kinds of economy in all periods of history. It was in fact a popular saying of the time; it reflects the popular wisdom of the day. It appears repeatedly in the gospels. In this instance Jesus is applying it to the process of understanding, and indeed we have already stressed that the same dynamic applies to all sorts of social and other processes. In Matthew 25:29 the dictum is directly applied to an economic issue.[5] I choose to open this section with Matt. 13:12 because it mentions not just abundance but superabundance, having more than one knows what to do with. The rich become rich to excess.

John Woolman links the economy directly to war: "Wealth is attended with power, by which bargains contrary to universal righteousness are supported; and here oppression ... becomes like a seed of discord in the soil; and ... swells and sprouts and grows and becomes strong, till much fruits are ripened."[6]

Myrdal breaks down the mechanism described in the dictum into two movements: the backwash and spread effects.

The backwash effect

The rich do not grow richer while coincidentally the poor grow poorer. The one causes the other; the rich grow richer at the expense of the poor. Imagine an area in which everyone is equally prosperous. As a result of some event, one place within the area becomes more prosperous than the rest. It attracts various factors of production. Since it offers investment opportunities, capital flows toward it, as do entrepreneurial spirits with ideas. Labour flows along with them since new jobs and higher pay are to be found there. All this increases income and opportunities that strengthen the appeal of the place. Meanwhile of course, the brighter, more adventurous people are leaving the periphery to seek their fortune in the new centre, especially since bright ideas are stimulated by the excitement of the place. People in the periphery with capital to spare see the advantage of investing it in the centre, where the prospects of profit are more promising, so that the periphery is starved of new investment. In many economic activities there are economies of scale. The greater the need for services like health or education, the cheaper it is to expand them. People in search of them will find a better range of them at a lower cost in the centre, making it ever more attractive. As education, for instance, improves in the centre, the children fortunate enough to grow up there will be better educated than their country cousins and will thus be better fitted to exploit the opportunities they find or which their skills make it easier for them to develop.

All in all, the centre sucks life out of the periphery.

That illustration is geographical. The same argument can be applied to class or social situation. The children of the rich have access to greater formal and informal educational opportunities; their playmates, classmates, and neighbours are advantaged in the same way. Thus they have access to a better network of people who can advise them, offer them jobs, or point them in the way of opportunities. They will not suffer the humiliations of being regarded as inferior, which in itself drives them to regard themselves as inferior and behave in consequence. Better educated as to what makes for good health and better able to afford it, they are likely to be more effective in their work and to live longer.[7] Wheels within wheels: since there is more profit to be made in selling cures for the illnesses of the rich than for those of the poor, pharmaceutical research concentrates on the former. As a result, the health and life expectancy of the rich continues to improve relative to that of the poor, since the medicines to treat the latter's illnesses are simply not being developed.

It is this sort of understanding of how the economy works that led one of the fathers of the church to say, "If you have two pairs of sandals and your neighbour has none, you must not give him a pair, but return it to him." The rich are the beneficiaries of a social process that has dispossessed the poor. That is not necessarily a matter for personal blame—it depends on the degree to which they have consciously manipulated the process to their advantage—but in any event, fairness calls for countervailing measures.

Spread effects

The centre generates not only backwash, but also spread effects that function in an opposite manner. The prosperous centre attracts workers who settle in the neighbourhood and places of work, which also scatter into neighbouring areas. In so far as people, enterprises, and public authorities spend where they are, a range of activities develops to meet their on-the-spot needs. Prosperity spreads outwards, but more thinly the further it gets from its source. At a certain distance, the spread effects are outweighed by the backwash effects. In spatial distribution, the former mitigates the latter without abolishing it.

The area that benefits from the spread effects may not be spatially continuous. For instance, the commuter travel network may create an archipelago of secondary centres depending on its particular characteristics. Thus, the high-speed train network in France has led to the growth of a number of suburbs of Paris, each with its own set of induced spread effects, around railway stations that are far from the capital in distance but close in travel time. Further afield, the demand in prosperous centres for goods that can only be produced in particular locations also gives rise to a sort of spotty spread effect. One thinks of oilfields, mines, seaside or mountain resorts, or the vineyards of Bordeaux.

Peaceable economies cultivate their spread effects.

The jubilee

The biblical sabbatical and jubilee years illustrate the same kind of mechanism with its backwash effects.[8] The model contains three elements or episodes (which in turn rest on a fourth, the sabbath): i) debts are written off; ii) slaves are freed; iii) and the land is returned to its original owners. The three elements are tied to each other in a single scenario that describes a common situation in peasant societies. Imagine a peasant family that is just able to make ends meet. Something goes awry: the rains fail, or a member of the family falls ill and is unable, even if only temporarily, to participate as expected in the family workforce. Ends no longer meet. To survive, the family has no choice but to borrow. Before, it could only just make ends meet. Now, on top of having to work flat out to survive, it has to service the debt. That is, of course, beyond its means. It is driven to selling off part of its land. Since at the outset it had only just enough land to meet its survival needs, it no longer has any prospect of viability now. It sinks into more and more debt and loses more and more of its land. In the end the only recourse that would have remained in the social conditions of the Middle East of biblical times was for the family to sell itself into slavery. Such an outcome still occurs in some places today, for instance with debt bondage in South Asia. The rich thus grow richer while the poor are reduced to utter destitution.

The model of the sabbatical year (every seventh year) and the jubilee (after seven times seven years, or roughly speaking a lifetime) restores the original situation. Debts are written off every seventh year: "Every seventh year you shall grant a remission of debts. And this is the manner of the remission: every creditor shall remit the claim that is held against a neighbor, not exacting it of a neighbor who is a member of the community" (Deut. 15:1-2).

Every seven years certain slaves are also freed:

If a member of your community, whether a Hebrew man or a Hebrew woman, is sold to you and works for you six years, in the seventh year you shall set that person free. And when you send a slave out from you a free person, you shall not send him out empty-handed. Provide liberally out of your flock, your threshing floor, and your wine press, thus giving to him some of the bounty with which the Lord your God has blessed you. Remember that you were a slave in the land of Egypt, and the Lord your God redeemed you; for this reason I lay this command upon you today. (Deut. 15:12-15)

To these two provisions, the Jubilee adds the return of property to its earlier owner. If anyone of your kin falls into difficulty and sells a piece of property . . . [and] if there are not sufficient means to recover it, what was sold shall remain with the purchaser until the year of jubilee; in the jubilee it shall be released, and the property shall be returned" (Lev. 25:25, 28).

Leviticus 25 also orders the liberation of slaves in the Jubilee year. "If any who are dependent on you become so impoverished that they sell themselves to you . . . They shall serve with you until the year of the jubilee. Then they and their children with them shall be free from your authority; they shall go back to their own family and return to their ancestral property" (Lev. 25:39-41).

After the debts are written off, the slaves are freed and return home to the land that has been returned to them. The peasant family once more is just able to make ends meet. What happens next? The system sets off again for another round. Hence the need to repeat the process regularly, again and again.

Deuteronomy 15 makes the point quite wittily. In verses 4 and 5 it declares there "There will, however, be no one in need among you, because the Lord is sure to bless you in the land that the Lord your God is giving you as a possession to occupy, if only you will obey the Lord your God by diligently observing this entire commandment that I command you today." Yet verse 11 flatly states, "For there will never cease to be some in need among you." The cycle thus never ceases. Admittedly, another interpretation may be entertained: that people will never be able to live up to the whole commandment. In fact the two interpretations are virtually the same.

One way of counteracting the ineluctable tendency for wealth and poverty to grow hand in hand is to reverse the process by restoring to the poor that which the grinding of the machine has taken from them and delivered to the rich. This process is often treated as if it were a matter of personal charity, gratuitous even when generous. It is much more than that; it is essential to maintaining the cohesion of society. It is part of the machinery. Without it society falls apart. One can compare the way an economy works to the action of a kitchen mixer. It takes the material in the centre of the bowl and throws it to the edge. The material needs to be constantly scraped off and brought back to the middle. Industrial mixers have built-in scrapers for this purpose. In the same way, the marginalized and excluded need to be folded back into the mix. There will always be some who are thrown to the margins, but if the mixer is working as it ought, it will not always be the same ones, and no one will remain permanently stuck at the edge.

Charity is better than nothing. It may even be the best available option when collective institutions are weak or missing. But it has the drawback of imposing the burden of maintaining the integrity of society disproportionately on the generous or those who can be made to feel guilty, even though people with that kind of character are no more responsible for the intrinsic workings of the economy than the thick-skinned and greedy.

Social policy can be fairer and more effective by combining equitable and inescapable taxes or other social charges with properly targeted expenditure, not just transfer payments but expenditure on collective services like public health or participatory democracy, or services with positive externalities for the poor like those that promote social mobility.

To do all the commandment asks does not come naturally. To reach out and fold the marginalized back into the system is just as counter-intuitive as to turn the other cheek, or to love one's enemy, which are corresponding responses to the same single dynamic of cumulative causation.

The Sabbath

The Sabbath is the starting point of all the foregoing biblical precepts. The sabbatical year is a Sabbath for the land (Lev. 25:4) and the jubilee is a Sabbath of sabbatical years (Lev. 25:8).

> Observe the sabbath day and keep it holy, as the Lord your God commanded you. Six days you shall labor and do all your work. But the seventh day is a sabbath to the Lord your God; you shall not do any work — you, or your son or your daughter, or your male or female slave, or your ox or your donkey, or any of your livestock, or the resident alien in your towns, so that your male and female slave may rest as well as you. (Deut. 5:12-14)

The Bible provides two kinds of argument for the Sabbath. The first is that it allows a respite in a life of hard work. Exodus 20:6-8 justifies it by recalling the statement in Genesis: "So God blessed the seventh day and hallowed it, because on it God rested from all the work that he had done in creation" (Gen. 2:3). The second argument is that the Sabbath provides liberation from servitude to production and productivism. Deuteronomy, while insisting that one's household, including one's domestic animals, are entitled to the Sabbath rest, adds: Remember that you were a slave in the land of Egypt, and the Lord your God brought you out from there with a mighty hand and an outstretched arm; therefore the Lord your God commanded you to keep the sabbath day" (Deut. 5:15).

Both the arguments for the Sabbath, rest and liberation, involve the economy of enough. They call on people to moderate their wants, to set limits to them. James takes the argument further, describing the consequences of unrestrained desires in the terms of the peaceable economy that concern us directly here.

The King James Version captures all this dramatically, pithily conflating individual and structural violence on the one hand and war and the economy on the other: "From whence come wars and fightings among you? Come they not hence, even of your lusts that war in your members? Ye lust, and have not: ye kill, and desire to have, and cannot obtain: ye fight and war, yet ye have not…" (James 4:1-2). Woolman illustrates how emulation turns an individual vice into a cumulative social process: "One person in society draws others into connection with him; and where these embrace the way this first hath chosen, their proceedings are like a wild vine which, springing from a single seed and growing strong, the branches extend, and their little twining holders twists round all herbs and boughs of trees where they reach."[9]

The jubilee sets the counters back to zero, ready for a fresh start. The Sabbath ideal is less radical, but at least it takes some steam out of the machine.

Big Ones and Little Ones, They All Fit In

The characteristics described so far apply to economies of any scale. They can apply to the global economy as a whole, as Lenin illustrated in his *Imperialism, the Highest Stage of Capitalism.*[10] The debate about dependency and centre-periphery relations in the global economy continued throughout most of the 20th century. Latterly it focused to an important degree in UNCTAD, the United Nations Conference on Trade and Development, founded for that purpose in 1964. Raúl Prebisch, one of the pioneers of dependency theory, became the first secretary-general of UNCTAD.[11] In an earlier period, mercantilism and its attendant imperialism had been the normal approach to the global economy. The policy was explicitly designed to exploit the periphery through a warlike combination of exclusion and domination, with or without military support.

The long debate about dependency still echoes in the controversy around the reference to "empire" in paragraph 19 of the Accra Confession of the then World Alliance of Reformed Churches (2004):

[W]e reject the current world economic order imposed by global neoliberal capitalism and any other economic system, including absolute planned economies, which defy God's covenant by excluding the poor, the vulnerable and the whole of creation from the fullness of life. We reject any claim of economic, political, and military empire which subverts God's sovereignty over life and acts contrary to God's just rule.

The art of those on the periphery was to place themselves inside the barriers and near enough to the centre to benefit more from its spread effects than suffer from its backwash effects. By and large, in the English-speaking world the "white Commonwealth" was especially successful in this regard during the imperial period.

The same process applies at the national level. Karl Marx was basically describing the workings of national economies in his *Capital*,[12] even if the class structures on which his analysis rests are international. Myrdal's model of the workings of economies sprang from his study of what he called "the Negro problem" in the United States.[13]

The process applies at the local level as well. The interplay of spread and backwash effects is evident in the geography of cities and their periphery. Calvin's path-breaking insights into the nascent capitalist economy sprang largely from his experience of Geneva, a town of under 10,000 people at the time of his arrival, with a peak around 25,000 around 1559.[14]

Many of his observations concern enterprises rather than geographical areas.

The features singled out in this book are found in economies of all sorts, as the paragraph of the Accra Confession quoted above also remarks. They could be found even inside a single village community well within the bounds of the subsistence affluence part of the economy of Fiji around 1970 (Subsistence affluence describes those parts of the economies of Pacific islands that generate an impressive level of health and prosperity without recourse to money). The features in question are even more evident in this kind of economy in their relations with the wider economy.[15]

To recapitulate, the dynamic of cumulative processes accurately describes how conflict and economies of any kind both work. The sociology of the Bible rests firmly on this model. It is realistic. In both economics and the management of conflict it offers a workable tool.

3. The Economy and the Law

When it comes to practical affairs, John Calvin has a pragmatic view of how laws function. In his Letter to Claude de Sachin on the legitimacy of charging interest, he says "let us not consider what is allowable in terms of received common custom, nor assess what is right and fair by the iniquitous standards of the world, but let us use the Word of God as a precept. . . . Let us not break the standard that the civil laws of the region or locality allow—though that is not always enough, because these laws permit things that they would not be able to correct or suppress by forbidding them. So we have to prefer fairness, which cuts back on excesses."[1] He is making two complementary points. Firstly, as Biéler points out, "positive laws represent the standards that a specific society constituted by sinful human beings gives itself to ensure the relative minimum order it needs to survive. Christians could never rest content with these inferior standards to regulate their behaviour."[2] Secondly, the laws may be intended to serve the particular interests of powerful groups, regardless of the public interest and especially of the interests of the weak and powerless.

The law often remains silent about behaviour which society generally regards as reprehensible, on the practical grounds that a law to repress it would be unenforceable. The converse is also true: authorities pass laws which they have no intention of enforcing, simply for show. In short, the law throws a spanner in the works, interfering with the unimpeded functioning of the lusts and warring which James denounces.[3]

The law is part of the institutional environment of the economy. It is one of the factors economic agents need to take into account in deciding on their course of action. The law forbids particular forms of behaviour and renders others obligatory. The law can serve as a constraint, an opportunity, or an obstacle to be got around.

Law-abiding people, firms, and public authorities take the law as setting limits to what they do, drawing boundaries to acceptable behaviour. In this spirit, for instance, the Nestlé Code of Business Conduct uncompromisingly proclaims the company's respect for the law. It: "We respect the law at all times. Nestlé and its employees are bound by the law. Compliance with all applicable laws and regulations must never be compromised."[4]

Economics as taught in universities tends to assume that economic agents are law-abiding, or even that laws passed by law makers are as inescapable as natural laws. That should be added to the list of unrealistic assumptions on which economics all too often rests. Sociologists have fewer scruples about treating the relationship to the law as just one factor among others in decision making. If economists were scientists objectively interested in economic behaviour, they would explore the costs and benefits of respecting, breaking, or dodging the law, or of engaging costs to bring about laws favourable to one's own interests. This would not be politically correct, however, and economists attach great weight to orthodoxy. In any event, the teachers are perfectly aware that the students are quite capable of taking the underlying economic models and applying them to conditions in which breaking the law is a conceivable choice, rationally calculating its expected costs and benefits. Calvin describes such an attitude in what he calls the second function of the law:

> The second function of the law is, for those who are concerned to do the right thing only when under constraint, that when they hear the fearful threats it contains, at least the dread of punishment will curb their wickedness. Such persons are curbed not because their heart is inwardly moved and affected, but they do not carry out their wicked desires because they are restrained as if by a bridle. Otherwise they would accomplish them in unbounded license. They are not better people on this account.[5]

Fear of punishment does not always have such a salutary effect, the less so the less the chance of being caught. Society has a corresponding economic decision to take: How much should it invest in making lawbreaking unprofitable? Or conversely: How much lawbreaking is it willing to accept, and of what kinds, as the price of not spending on law-enforcement?

By establishing boundaries and setting constraints, the law affects relative costs and prices. Its transgression can thus provide tempting economic opportunities, such as tax evasion (including smuggling in the days when customs and excise had an important effect on prices); blackmail; illegal trade (in arms or drugs for instance); and fraud, mislabelling, or adulterating goods. Laws and rules create countless opportunities for engaging lucratively in bribery and corruption, both actively and passively (Active corruption corresponds to paying a bribe; passive corruption to receiving one). Paradoxically, in some cases spending more on law enforcement can increase the profitability of lawbreaking by rendering access too costly for small fry. In all these cases, if the law were repealed, the source of profit would dry up. For the *homines œconomici* of economic theory, the decision whether or not to respect the law is an economic decision like any other. Theory says they should choose whichever is the more remunerative, regardless of any ethical or moral considerations. The range of choices includes pretending to obey the law while actually breaking it. Deception is an option in the economy as in war (cf. pp. 39-41).

The foregoing passage deals with decision makers who have the means to take economic decisions coolly. That situation is a luxury for the most deprived, whose needs are immediate. Their very lives are at stake. They have no choice but to break laws imposed by the rich to protect their own property. Indeed they are entitled to break such illegitimate laws. As *Gaudium et spes* puts it, "If one is in extreme necessity, one has the right to procure for oneself what one needs out of the riches of others."[6]

Legitimacy and the Law

The law is more likely to be respected if it is regarded as legitimate. The legitimacy may stem from social conventions. As we have seen, Calvin warns against bowing too readily to such conventions. The converse can be equally true: laws may forbid things that meet the needs of the deprived or the requirements of human dignity and human rights: in a word, whatever the love of one's neighbour demands. In such cases also, we have to prefer fairness.

The code of conduct of the transnational corporation BP explicitly recognizes the complexity of the issue of respecting both the law and social norms. It states in its code of conduct:

What about different laws in different countries? BP does business globally, and that means our employees are subject to the laws and regulations of different countries, and of organizations such as the European Union (EU). Each of us is responsible for knowing and following the laws that apply to us where we work. The [BP code of conduct] establishes principles for business conduct applicable throughout the group, regardless of location. Where differences exist as the result of local customs, norms, laws or regulations, you must apply either the code or local requirements—whichever sets the highest standard of behaviour.[7]

BP thus explicitly recognizes that its employees ultimately come face to face with their own consciences. This touchstone of legitimacy can bring into play what Calvin calls the third function of the law:

The third use of the law, which is its main one and which properly belongs to the purpose for which it has been given, has its place among the faithful in whose hearts the Spirit of God already flourishes and reigns … It is a very good instrument for enabling them day by day to learn better and with greater certainty what is the will of the Lord which they aspire to follow.[8]

The second and third functions of the law actually refer to two different kinds of law. The former kind consists of laws passed by political authorities, while the latter are the dictates of conscience. However, when all is said and done, it is the bridle of conscience—whether aided or hindered by the conventions that are part of belonging to a given community—that determines how far laws and rules are respected. Indeed flagrant violation of a law can be a way of marking one's membership of a group. Ah, the pleasure and complicity of little transgressions!

Economists happily preach about proper behaviour—that is, rational according to their models. They make no bones about urging the authorities to adopt laws in conformity with the economists' view of what the natural laws are, because it would be futile to pass laws in conflict with nature as they perceive it. What a pity that the laws of economics are less self-evident than the laws that say that rivers don't flow uphill.

The struggle for legitimacy against legality in the economy can lead, on the other hand, to serious open conflict. Gandhi's Salt March of 1930 is an epic model. It was initiated by a letter from Gandhi to the Viceroy of India:

> If my letter makes no appeal to your heart, on the eleventh day of this month I shall proceed with such co-workers of the Ashram as I can take, to disregard the provisions of the

Salt Laws. I regard this tax to be the most iniquitous of all from the poor man's standpoint. As the Independence movement is essentially for the poorest in the land, the beginning will be made with this evil.

This particular incident ended with over 50, 000 people in jail.

Law and War

Law and war are independent of each other. Laws are often broken in peace time. Indeed, as we have seen, breaking the law is normal behaviour for the *homo œconomicus* of economic theory, since this actor is not equipped with a conscience. On the other hand, war has its laws. It is often in the interest of the belligerents to respect them. However, they are also often broken because one or other of the belligerents expects to gain thereby, or because they get carried away by the internal dynamics of the essential nastiness of war.

4. Violence in War and the Economy

The pivot between violence and the economy lies in the eighth commandment, which is commonly rendered as "Thou shalt not steal," but which also conveys the meaning "thou shalt kidnap no-one,"[1] or thou shalt deprive no one of their freedom of action. Depriving someone of their goods is clearly an economic matter, but depriving them of their means of action is a broader form of violence that includes it. Violence is embedded in the economy.

As a social phenomenon in general, violence involves putting people into a position they would not freely choose. The source of the violence may be individual or structural, the latter being defined as being beyond the control of any individual.

War, defined as "an act of force to compel our enemy to do our will,"[2] is no more than a special form of violence. It is still a violation of the eighth commandment. If this chapter focuses on war, it is simply to emphasize the characteristics of violence by focusing on a particularly clear expression of it.

The Nature of War

With respect to the philosophy of war, Carl von Clausewitz (1780–1831) dominates the field with his monumental work *On War*, published posthumously in 1832. The Chinese thinker on war Sun Tzu ranks almost as highly in authority and prestige. He would have been writing in the 5th century BCE, although there is some doubt about Sun Tzu's identity, or even his existence as a historical figure.

Clausewitz gives two definitions of war. The first is "War is an act of force to compel our enemy to do our will." His paradigm was an armed conflict between two nation states. The enemy was thus undoubtedly an alien and was going to remain one. Sun Tzu's paradigm was different: it involved wars of conquest within China. The adversaries, once defeated, would become subjects, and their economy would be incorporated into the victor's possessions. Sun Tzu was therefore more concerned than Clausewitz to preserve the adversaries and their resources. Ideally, the opponent should be brought to submission without fighting at all. "The skilful leader subdues the enemy's troops without any fighting."[3] This has passed into broader use along the lines of, "The art of war is to subdue the enemy without fighting."

Sun Tzu was conscious of the dynamics of emotions. He warned against massacres and atrocities because of the reactions of enmity and hatred they can provoke, which might even turn the tide of war against the perpetrators.

Clausewitz's second description, if not definition, of war is generally cited in a truncated or even modified form such as, "War is the continuation of policy [or politics] by other means." A more accurate rendering is "War is simply the continuation of political intercourse with the addition of other means." Clausewitz continues: "We deliberately use the phrase "with the addition of other means" because we also want to make it clear that war in itself does not suspend political intercourse or change it into something entirely different."[4]

War and economics share an identical framework of rationality. Sun Tzu's *Art of War* is often used in management courses because so much of it applies to business. In both war and economics, rationality involves investing as little as possible to achieve a given end. The 20 precepts that make up Chapter 2 of the 13 chapters of Sun Tzu's *Art of War* are more or less entirely devoted to recommendations on the economics of waging war (Sun Tzu's treatise is exemplary in its brevity[5]).

Two of the defining characteristics of war are violence and the existence of an enemy. Most forms of economic organization involve violence, even when they cause less bloodshed than war.

The opponents in war are normally called enemies; in the economy they are often described as rivals or competitors, but these terms can mislead one into forgetting most of the contestants. Economic agents hope to benefit from the terms of their exchange with suppliers, workers, customers, the general public, and others, even, but not always, at their expense.

The difference between rivals and enemies is not necessarily great. Rivals compete with each other while enemies are hostile to each other. This distinction, drawn from the *Concise Oxford Dictionary*, is not all that helpful as the same dictionary defines "hostile" as "of an enemy" or "opposed." The key lies in a third expression it uses, "unfriendly." Rivals can be friends, and they often are. In sports in which opponents confront each other, like tennis or football, opponents are indispensable, and the more equal the rivals' skill, the more fun the game is.

Friendship between enemies is not unknown even in war. This can on occasion be subsumed under the Marxist concept of class war. The officer class recognizes its own even among the enemy. Enmity also exists in the economy. The personnel of one enterprise can murder that of another, as occurs in the drug trade or in Mafia-type territorial conflicts. And there are countless instances of employers instigating the murder of workers.

There is a grey area in which war and the economy overlap. Militias, not to mention the official armed forces themselves, assassinate their own economic opponents or those of their employers. We see this, for instance, in the untimely deaths of trade unionists or leaders of peasant or indigenous movements or those who speak for them.

One of the usual purposes of war is to subject a community or social group. For Sun Tzu, this was the normal case. The aim in such a situation is not to annihilate the enemy, but to bring it to acquiesce in a different state of affairs. In market economies, too, employers and workers engage in a perpetual tug of war, each trying to obtain, at the expense of the other, a greater share of the output of the enterprise of which they are both stakeholders. Neither, however, wishes the disappearance of the other, since they cannot survive without each other. Employers long for a docile work force that does not push its claims too firmly.

And then, of course, there is war as business, epitomized by mercenary enterprises and private security firms active in war, not to mention the military-industrial complex.[6]

On the other side, economic activity does not require an enemy or even a rival. The victims of economic activities are often collateral. The harm they suffer is not always intentional. It may be that the chain of cause and effect is not understood. Decision makers may be using a faulty or inappropriate model. The ramifications of their action may be so extensive that they have not fully examined them.

It may even be that the decision makers have decided that the victims got what they deserve. Here we enter the realm of racism, xenophobia, caste, or class privilege. In such cases, the victim is indeed seen as an enemy. There are those who claim that if the unemployed cannot find work, it is their own fault, or that people who have failed to cope with the stress of their job have flawed characters. There are those who insist that the streets be cleared of beggars without proposing any alternative means of livelihood to them. Such people are not ignoring the victims of the economy; they are designating them as enemies.

Hostility involves emotions. Not everyone feels a need to construct a rational explanation for their dislikes. Those who do rationalize them may well resort to a model that does not correspond to reality, or that corresponds to the wrong part of reality. Thus, for instance, those who argue that the unemployed are lazy may be using a microeconomic model about individual decisions when the issue is macroeconomic and concerns overall effective demand. Or, given that employers are not offering enough jobs to go around, they are assuming that everyone is capable of setting up their own enterprise and thus becoming self-employed. Their model leaves out the diversity of gifts that is a characteristic of human nature (1 Cor. 12:4). Calvin stresses that the passage applies not just to spiritual gifts, "but in all the branches of knowledge which come into use in common life."[7]

In both war and economics, however, the internal dynamics of the processes involved can take control, even leading the participants to lose sight of their initial aim. Rationality may be swamped by other factors.

Is War a Science?

While conventional wisdom considers economics to be a science, it equally readily considers war to be an art. That was already Sun Tzu's view 2500 years ago; his treatise even bears the title *The Art of War*. Two factors weigh heavily in the decision to classify it as an art.

The first is the "fog of war." The phrase was coined by Clausewitz: "War is the domain of uncertainty; three quarters of the things on which all action in war is based are lying in a fog of uncertainty to a greater or lesser extent."[8] Partial or unreliable information are facts of life. In war they are aggravated by deliberate efforts to deceive the enemy, as Sun Tzu stressed.[9] Deliberate deception plays its part in the economy as well, as Bernard Madoff, a US financier convicted in 2009 of a vast international fraud extending over several years, will confirm; but even in the absence of deception, economic agents have to take decisions in conditions of poor information.

The second factor is what Clausewitz called "friction." In schoolbook physics, as in elementary economics, theory describes a world free from friction. Friction separates reality from theory. The idea of friction warns decision makers to give full weight to reality in all its complexity; it warns them against being carried away by the elegance of coherent logical models alone. Unlike the science of economics, the art of war is alert to friction. Clausewitz insisted bluntly on its importance when he advised, "No plan survives the first contact with the enemy."[10] The "enemy" here represents reality.

It is of course incorrect to think that science or economics ignore friction. The aim of science being to explain reality, it must build friction into its models. The models that ignore it are conscious simplifications designed to focus attention for the purposes of a particular argument on selected aspects of the process under examination. Economics, on the other hand, all too often fails to build all the asperities of reality back into its models when the time comes.

Here then are two useful things that the science of economics can learn from the art of war. If taking fog and friction into account is what distinguishes an art from a science, economics would be better off as an art.

Warlike Economies

The conduct of war and economic activities share a number of techniques. This section will explore a few of them.

Correct information

Sun Tzu insists that deception is at the heart of warfare. It is no less deeply rooted in the workings of the economy. "Can I tolerate wicked scales and a bag of dishonest weights? Your wealthy are full of violence; your inhabitants speak lies, with tongues of deceit in their mouths" (Micah 6:11-12). On the other hand, deception is not at the heart of the economy;

there it is only an occasional possibility. Although it is sensible to check what one is told, society and the economy would be unworkable if trust were not the default position.

Note that Micah regards deceitful weights as a form of violence. Here too, war and the economy embrace.

Devise unfathomable plans.[11]

Secrecy, a normal constituent of the military mentality, has always been a standard feature of the market economy. At the World Trade Organization (WTO), the US has argued that to require that customers be informed about what they are buying is an obstacle to trade.

Intellectual property is gaining considerable importance in today's market economy. Knowledge becomes private property to be bought and sold—and protected. To achieve that, free access must be denied.

> As stated in Article 27 of the Universal Declaration of Human Rights, the right to enjoy the benefits of scientific advancement and the right to the protection of the interests resulting from one's own scientific production have to be balanced. This equilibrium is not easy to attain … [A] difficulty concerned the opinion of a project partner that research results coming from publicly financed research must remain public. This perspective would be sustainable in a perfect world. However, confronted with

current [intellectual property] legislation and the importance of knowledge-based economies, if a publicly funded research centre does not claim its own research results, the work and investment of many years could be exploited by others.[12]

Some trade secrets, like the ingredients of Chanel No. 5, make life more fun. A moral problem arises with secrecy in intellectual property rights when it has more far-reaching social and economic implications. If scientific research that affects the public interest is funded and guarded by profit-oriented enterprises, the institutional arrangements will encourage them to concentrate their efforts on areas that have the best prospects of profit rather than those of greatest public interest. Pharmaceutical research is an example that is currently the object of considerable debate.

Unfathomable plans in the form of algorithms so complicated that even their users couldn't fathom them, not to mention their supervisors, were the triumph of the financial system in the crisis that started around 2008. They worked like a charm. Banks put themselves into an unacceptable financial state by using such devices. Governments felt compelled to bail them out with massive injections of taxpayers' money. The public was reduced to paying tribute to the victorious financial sector. Sun Tzu would have applauded. "To fight and conquer in all your battles is not supreme excellence; supreme excellence consists in breaking the enemy's resistance without fighting."[13] The banks obtained huge public subsidies without fighting.

Practise deception.

Withholding information, providing misleading information, and otherwise manipulating one's interlocutor's state of mind are the stock-in-trade of psychological warfare. As any specialist in advertising or public relations will confirm, they are equally normal tools of marketing. Four and a half centuries ago, Calvin was already able to describe them accurately (Box p. 79ss, §45).

At least one further form of manipulation needs to be added to Calvin's list, but it is a crucial one: to flaunt mendacious models of reality in order to convince one's opposite number to hand over what is rightfully theirs. The economic model describing the economy as a system in stable equilibrium that will spontaneously return to its original position if it is disturbed is a case in point. If that were the way the economy worked, there would be no point in attempting to correct the hardships it inflicts on the poor and the defenceless because any such effort would be futile. The weak would have to resign themselves to bearing the weight that the market presses on them. There is nothing to be said either for or against those who amass wealth and power. As the former British Prime Minister Margaret Thatcher, a champion of neo-liberalism, put it, "There is no alternative." Isaiah must have had it all wrong when he upbraided you who join house to house, who add field to field, until there is room for no one but you, and you are left to live alone in the midst of the land!" (Is. 5:8). The neo-liberal model is a subterfuge that the rich use to bamboozle the poor.

Freedom

Buyers and sellers need to be free to accept or reject any offer made by the other. As the saying goes, transactions must in that sense be "at arm's length." The object of war is to reduce one's enemy to a state of dependency, to deprive it of the capacity to act freely. Similarly, buyer and seller in the market strive to reduce the capacity of the other party to act freely. Fostering brand loyalty is one means among many, eliminating one's competitors is another. If one party is in debt to the other, it is thereby in the other's grip.

While buyer and seller are struggling to ensnare each other, they share a common interest in reducing the freedom of the rest of society in relation to their trades. In so far as they can transfer their costs onto the rest of society, they both gain—or at least they can fight over how to share between them the gain they have jointly appropriated at the expense of others. Thus consumers and sellers of petrol, not to mention the manufacturers of motor vehicles, benefit by unloading the environmental costs of air pollution or global warming onto others. Since buyers and sellers are likely to be fewer in number and better organized than the public at large, they are generally in a stronger position to press home their advantage. Those who are affected may not even realize what is going on: Calvin explicitly mentioned that too (Box p. 79ss, §45). That is why the retail price of petrol, for example, nowhere covers the total costs incurred by its use. The same is true for nuclear energy and other activities that discharge harmful wastes into the environment.

Freedom from the pressure of time is also inequitably distributed: James states, "Behold, the hire of the labourers who have reaped your fields, which is kept back by you, crieth, and the cries . . . are entered into the ears of the Lord of sabaoth" (James 5:4). The Lord of sabaoth is the Lord of hosts: that is, of the armies. The image is a military one of the mighty God marching to restore a fair balance of power (compare Ps. 89: 8,10: "O Lord God of hosts, who is as mighty as you, O Lord? . . . you scattered your enemies with your mighty arm.") "Sabaoth" is a strong word, underlining the gravity of the offence.

James is not even complaining that the workers are not being paid, but that their employer is slow to pay them. The workers need their wages without delay so that their families can buy what they need for supper that same evening. The market seller needs to sell her carrots before they go bad (Photo p. 89).

The rich by definition have reserves. Those who have reserves can wait to pounce until the moment most favourable to themselves. "The wealth of the rich is their fortress; the poverty of the poor is their ruin" (Prov. 10:15). The rich can shelter out of reach behind their wealth, and at a moment of their own choosing sally forth to lay waste the surrounding countryside. "The ruin of the poor" ingeniously carries two meanings. One the one hand, their poverty leads to their ruin, to even worse poverty; on the other, the poor have only a ruin for shelter and it is of course no match.

Calvin described the relationship in his usual highly imaged manner. It is worth quoting at length:

> When a rich person has goods to trade, when someone comes to him he will say "You will not have it for less". Why that? His wares do not diminish in his shop; but if there is a poor person earning his living one day at a time, who hasn't a penny to his name, he will be forced to sell what he has at an insulting price. Buying in these conditions, well aware of the pressure the seller is under, is clearly oppression, and we can say, as the proverb puts it, this is to put one's foot on his throat—it is a kind of brigandry. That, I say, is what one would say when someone buys from those in want who are so constrained that they are at wit's end, and have no other resource than to do what they do not want to do. So let us note that God

did not only command paying those who have worked without letting them languish until the next day; he wished attention to be paid to each individual's indigence ... When we bargain, it should not be to say "take it or leave it."[14]

Is that not the very definition of war, "an act of force to compel our enemy to do our will?" The reformer's tone only echoes that of the prophet: "Alas for those who devise wickedness and evil deeds on their beds! When the morning dawns, they perform it, because it is in their power. They covet fields, and seize them; houses, and take them away" (Micah 2:1-2).

War against creation

The economy has striven since the beginnings of human society to bend its environment to its will. It has applied increasing amounts of energy to that end, which is not far from saying that it has used increasing violence. Humanity's relationship to the rest of creation thus resembles war according to Clausewitz' first definition.

The Old Testament, focusing on humanity's relations to animals,[15] describes a warlike situation. Genesis 1:26 talks only of dominion, which can be pacifically interpreted as governing like a well-intentioned lord. On the other hand, verse 28 talks of subduing the earth. It is trickier to give a peaceable turn to that phrase. In any event, between the creation and the flood, animals have had time to experience human dominion. God pointed out to Noah and his sons as they were preparing to leave the Ark, "the fear of you and the dread of you shall rest on every animal of the earth." Worse still, he added that "every moving thing that lives shall be food for you" (Gen. 9:2-3), a fate from which they were explicitly spared in Gen. 1:29.

In the course of history, humanity has treated the rest of creation like an enemy. But there is a difference: like the just in James 5:6, the environment does not strike back—that is the meaning of "resist"—at least not with intention. The environment simply adjusts to changes in its own environment. If that is inconvenient for humanity or some sections of it, that is no more than a coincidental side effect. The war between humanity and the rest of creation is at least free from the cumulative processes of revenge described in Chapter 2.

War against the understanding of reality

Reality is so rich and complex that humans can manage their life within it only by organizing the way they perceive it into simplified systematic models. Language classifies things into categories, grouping some together and distinguishing others. Classifications imply a view on relations of cause and effect, on sequences in time, and even on whether something has happened or not. Language is a fundamental tool in making sense of the world. In the story of Babel (Gen. 11:1-9), God confounded the single language of the world and scattered people over the face of all the earth. Different languages were created to make sense of the different environments in which they were to live. Language can be taken as shorthand for the whole structure of knowledge. In thus scattering the people, God opened the way for a diversity of visions of reality to meet a diversity of needs. On Pentecost however, everyone understands what everyone is saying, each in their own language (Acts 2:1-11). There is communication between the cultures without any one dominating the others.

There is no better way to get people to do your will than to persuade them that there is no alternative, that yours is the only conceivable form of truth. It is a Procrustian version of "one size fits all": everyone must be made to fit the only size provided. To convince people that yours is the only legitimate form of science, the only way of understanding reality, is to deny the culture of others, to make them feel ignorant and unworthy.

In today's market economy, science and business have leagued together to impose a single model of reality, to privatize it through the intellectual property system, and to draw profit from it. To protect one's knowledge against the inroads of international business one has to master the peculiar mumbo-jumbo, not to mention the institutional labyrinths, indispensable to patent or copyright it. It is a costly and culturally arcane process. It is furthermore founded on the notion of ownership of knowledge by individuals, companies, or other institutions recognized in the peculiar legal structures that govern swathes of the dominant economy, but not all parts of all economies.

In this war between knowledge systems, it is to the credit of the World Intellectual Property Organization (WIPO) that it does explicitly concern itself with "Traditional Knowledge, Genetic Resources and Traditional Cultural Expressions/ Folklore," seeking to take the interests of the communities concerned into account, albeit within the overall framework of the dominant business model.[16]

5. The Characteristics of Peaceable Economies

> We must relinquish the desire to own other people,
> to have power over them, and to force our views
> onto them.
> – Statement on peace issued by New Zealand
>   Quakers, 1987

To explore the nature of a peaceable economy, it is useful first to identify the warlike elements of economies. The most essential ones are implicit in Clausewitz' definition of war: "an act of force to compel our enemy to do our will." War involves violence, and it seeks to subdue the adversary, to impair their freedom of action, their capacity to do as they wish. These two defining characteristics of war are both widespread in economies.

Calvin also stresses the parallels between the features that war and the economy share in this regard. His arguments are summarized, fittingly, in his commentary on the commandments "Thou shalt not kill" (6th) and "Thou shalt not steal" (8th) in *The Institutes*. We are now skirmishing in the field of ethics, of how people ought to behave. Since the economy that economists study is not peaceable, we need to explore the changes in human behaviour required if it is to become peaceable. We are resolutely moving from description to sermon.

The pair "Thou shalt not kill" and "Thou shalt not steal" is even nearer to Clausewitz' definition of war if one bears in mind, as we explained at the start of Chapter 4, that the injunction normally translated into English by "Thou shalt not steal" is actually closer to "Thou shalt deprive no-one of the means to be in control of their own actions,"[1] For Gandhi (see box opposite), it is a matter of restoring people to control over their own life and destiny.[2] The key to the peaceable economy lies in the 6th commandment being thus understood. "Thou shalt not kill" is no more than a special case of the 8th.

It is worthwhile to examine Calvin's comments on these commandments in some detail. I shall also include some of his comments on the last commandment, "Thou shalt not covet," where he develops principles already explained in the previous two. The passages most pertinent for the present argument are reproduced in the box.

Gandhi's Talisman

I will give you a talisman. Whenever you are in doubt, or when the self becomes too much with you, apply the following test. Recall the face of the poorest and the weakest man [or woman] whom you may have seen, and ask yourself, if the step you contemplate is going to be of any use to him [or her]. Will he [or she] gain anything by it? Will it restore him [or her] to a control over his [or her] own life and destiny? In other words, will it lead to swaraj for the hungry and spiritually starving millions? Then you will find your doubts and your self melt away.

Calvin extends the meaning of "kill," "steal," and "covet" well beyond their literal or primary sense. He gives "the well-being and conservation of all must be considered as entrusted to each" as the purport of the 6th commandment, "we must render to every person their due" as that of the 8th; and "the sum [of the 10th] will be that no thought be permitted to insinuate itself into our minds and move our hearts to any desire involving trouble and cost for our neighbour." The injunction not "to destroy our neighbour in order to attract his goods to us" is included in the commentary on the 6th commandment, not the 8th. The meanings given to all three commandments are thus extremely close.

To underline further the extensive but single scope of the three, Calvin examines their opposite: if killing, stealing, and coveting are forbidden, than what is required of us as a consequence?

> If we can do anything to preserve the life of our neighbour, then we are required faithfully to do it, whether it be by bringing about whatever tends to that end or by obviating whatever is contrary to it; and if we do not strive according to our means and opportunity to do the right thing by our neighbour, by that cruelty we violate this precept [Thou shalt not kill]. The [8th] commandment forbids us to attract other people's goods to ourselves, and accordingly requires us to exert ourselves faithfully so that each person preserves their own. The 10th enjoins each person [to] exert their will to preserving and advancing what is beneficial and useful to every one.

The pair of words 'beneficial and useful' can be taken as a direct opposite to the pair 'trouble and cost' reproved in the same paragraph. The phrase also appears in the final sentence of the commentary on the 8th commandment.

Calvin returns repeatedly to the need to help and support the weaker members of the community, not merely through charity but also by offering sound advice.

> Let it be our constant aim faithfully to lend our counsel and aid to all so as to assist them in retaining what is theirs

... Let us contribute to the relief of those whom we see under the pressure of difficulties, assisting their want out of our abundance. Lastly, let each of us consider how far he is bound to others in the duty of his office, in order to carry it out in good faith, to help and support [our neighbour] if they are in any danger or perplexity.

This requirement surprisingly comes in the commentary on "Thou shalt not kill." It thus stresses how the purport of the commandment involves actively supporting the weaker members of the community when the difficulties of life are beyond them.

It should be stressed that, as the context makes clear, to "assist their want out of our abundance" is not just a matter of charity, of giving people things of which we have plenty. The abundance can extend to any resource, including experience, knowledge, influence and yet more.

Killing is a characteristic activity in war, where it is intentional or at least a consciously accepted consequence of belligerent action. Calvin stresses that the commandment can be violated without any intention to kill and even if no one is directly killed. "Whoever in act perpetrates ... anything which is contrary to the good of their neighbour, God regards as a murderer. Every kind of violence and offence and harm by which our neighbour's body suffers, is prohibited to us." The commandment embraces any violence intrinsic to a situation, and thus structural violence.

Calvin is at pains to stress that the scope of the 8th commandment is not restricted to depriving other people of their belongings. In a remarkably modern phrase, he adds that it "extends to every kind of right." This statement rests on the meaning underlying the word "steal" in the commandment. He goes on to underline the positive duty to which the commandment enjoins us: "We defraud our neighbours of what is theirs if we deny them any of the duties which we are bound to perform towards them."

In the illustrative list of forms of theft which Calvin provides, he includes deception: "There are many kinds of theft: … another in malicious imposture, when one craftily impoverishes one's neighbour by cheating and deception; yet another in flattery, which by honeyed words wiles away … that which should belong to someone else." For Sun Tzu, deception is at the heart of warfare.

Calvin also includes unjust law in his list: "an even more hidden craft which deprives someone of their possessions under cover of the law." This comes under the heading of compelling others to do our will, reducing others to subjection, one of the defining objectives of war.

Calvin ends his enumeration with the pithy "any means which we use to enrich ourselves at the expense of others should be regarded as theft." The whole of Calvin's argument in his commentary on the three commandments is summed up in the phrase "each person should exert their will to preserving and advancing what is beneficial and useful to every one." It describes win-win situations: everyone should come out better off. It is difficult, not to say impossible, to imagine win-win as a war aim in any conditions.

John Calvin
Institutes of the Christian Religion
Book 2, Chapter 8
Comments on the 6th, 8th, & 10th commandments

6th Commandment.
THOU SHALT NOT KILL.

39. The purport is that, since the Lord has joined in unity the whole of humanity, the well-being and conservation of all must be considered as entrusted to each. In short therefore, every kind of violence and offence and harm by which our neighbour's body suffers, is prohibited to us. Which brings us to the commandment, which is that if we can do anything to preserve the life of our neighbour, then we are required faithfully to do it, whether it be by bringing about whatever tends to that end or by obviating whatever is contrary to it; and in the same way to help and support them if they are in any danger or perplexity...

40. To be clear of the crime of murder, it is not enough to refrain from shedding blood. Whoever in act perpetrates, or in endeavour and design plots, or in

their heart conceives anything which is contrary to the good of their neighbour, God regards as a murderer. On the other hand, if we do not strive according to our means and opportunity to do the right thing by our neighbour, by that cruelty we violate this precept...

8th Commandment.
THOU SHALT NOT STEAL.

45. The purport is that, injustice being displeasing to God, we must render to every person their due. In short, then, the commandment forbids us to attract other people's goods to ourselves, and accordingly requires us to exert ourselves faithfully so that each person preserves their own... [O]ne cannot defraud anyone of their wealth without violating God's dispensation. There are many kinds of theft: one consists in violence, as when a person's goods are forcibly plundered and carried off as it were by brigandry; another in malicious imposture, when one craftily impoverishes one's neighbour by cheating and deception; a third in an even more hidden craft which deprives someone of their possessions under cover of the law; yet another in flattery, which by honeyed words wiles away under the pretence of donation or otherwise that which should belong to someone else. But not to dwell too long in enumerating the different kinds, let us simply note that any means which

we use to enrich ourselves at the expense of others should be regarded as theft ... No matter whether those who proceed in that kind of way often win their case before the judge, God will still regard them as none other than thieves, because he sees the ambushes clever people lay from afar to catch the simple in their nets, he sees the harshness of the exactions which the greater impose on the lesser to crush them, he sees how poisonous are the flatteries used by those who want to sweeten someone up to cheat them even if people don't notice ... Furthermore, the transgression of this precept is not just a matter or wronging someone with respect to their money, or merchandise, or possessions, but extends to every kind of right; for we defraud our neighbours of what is theirs if we deny them any of the duties which we are bound to perform towards them.

46. This commandment, therefore, we shall duly obey, if, contented with our own lot, we study to acquire nothing but by honest and legitimate gain; if we do not seek to grow rich by wronging our neighbour, nor to destroy our neighbour in order to attract his goods to us; if we do not study to assemble wealth from the blood and sweat of others; if we do not attract from here and there and by any means, whatever we can to glut our avarice or spend on superfluities. On the contrary, let it be our constant aim faithfully to lend our counsel and aid to all so as to assist them in

retaining what is theirs ... [L]et us contribute to the relief of those whom we see under the pressure of difficulties, assisting their want out of our abundance. Lastly, let each of us consider how far he is bound to others in the duty of his office, in order to carry it out in good faith ... Let every one, I say, thus consider what in his own place and order he owes to his neighbours, and render to them what he owes them[3] ... [E]ach person should exert their will to preserving and advancing what is beneficial and useful to every one.

10th Commandment.
THOU SHALT NOT COVET THY NEIGHBOUR'S HOUSE, THOU SHALT NOT COVET THY NEIGHBOUR'S WIFE NOR HIS MAN-SERVANT, NOR HIS MAID-SERVANT, NOR HIS OX NOR HIS ASS, NOR ANYTHING THAT IS THY NEIGHBOUR'S.

49. The purport is: Since the Lord would have the whole soul pervaded and possessed by the feeling of love,[4] we must throw out of our heart any contrary cupidity.[5] The sum, therefore, will be that no thought be permitted to insinuate itself into our minds and move our hearts to any desire involving trouble and cost for our neighbour. To this corresponds the opposite affirmative precept, that every thing which we conceive, deliberate, seek or pursue be at the same time beneficial and useful to our neighbour...

50. ...God therefore commands a strong and ardent love for our neighbour which is not to be impeded by any portion, however minute, of cupidity. He requires a heart so admirably arranged as not to be prompted in the slightest degree contrary to the law of love.

What Kind of Economy Is Peaceable?

We have seen how intimately the characteristics of war resemble those of the economy. Let us now take the opposite approach and try to describe the characteristics of a truly peaceable economy.

A freely chosen peacefulness

Its peace must be free. No one has been pressed into docility, reduced to resigning themselves to accepting a state of affairs because to contest it would only make things worse for themselves. Everyone is actually content with their position in the economy. It is a fair economy in that no one feels hard done by. That is a particular sense of a just economy, or indeed of a just peace. It should not however be confused with an economy that is considered just when measured by some externally determined yardstick.

There is still a hitch in this criterion. Maybe the contentment does not spring from a spontaneous modesty of desires; maybe people have been persuaded to be content in their station, even if an outside observer feels that it is one in which they are unfairly exploited.

In some churches there is a long tradition of preaching the virtues of humility. Thomas Aquinas defines humility as consisting "in keeping oneself within one's own bounds, not reaching out to things above one," But the sting is in the tail, since the sentence ends "submitting to one's superior."[6]
Preaching humility has an odd ring when those who are preaching it represent rich and powerful interests that can draw profit from an undemanding nature in their inferiors, tenants, employees, or others who depend on their decisions. Woolman states,

> Were all superfluities and the desire of outward greatness laid aside and the right use of things universally attended to, such a number of people might be employed in things useful that moderate labour with the blessing of heaven would answer all good purposes relating to people and their animals, and a sufficient number have leisure to attend on proper affairs of civil society.[7]

A peaceful but just economy requires not only that people be undemanding for themselves, but also that they be ceaselessly solicitous of the welfare of others, and in particular that those in positions of power be concerned for the empowerment of the powerless, including their political freedom as

Woolman explicitly points out. Neither of these characteristics comes naturally.

That is not far removed from the *swaraj* of Gandhi's Talisman. It is a complex and demanding concept. In what is undoubtedly an intentionally ambiguous phrase, Gandhi said, "It is swaraj when we learn to rule ourselves."[8]

"At the individual level, *swaraj* is vitally connected with the capacity for dispassionate self-assessment, ceaseless self-purification and growing self-reliance."[9] At the political level it is sovereignty of the people based on moral authority. It embodies an anarchist ideal; Gandhi had little faith in big government, be it colonial or independent. "In . . . a state [where *swaraj* is achieved] everyone is his own ruler. He rules himself in such a manner that he is never a hindrance to his neighbour."[10]

An Economy Free from Envy

Envy is absent in a truly peaceable economy. That does not however mean that people should not strive to model their behaviour, including their wants, on those of others. As Aristotle said, man is by nature a political animal: that is, designed to live in society.[11] That necessarily involves conforming one's life-style to that of the people among whom one is living because that is a way to mark belonging.

The danger to be avoided, as René Girard points out, is that role models can easily become the focus of envy, rivals to be outdone if not defeated.[12] We desire an object not for its own sake, but because we want to imitate the person who renders the object desirable by possessing it. In many cases indeed, the imitator does not want an object that is *like* the role model's, but wants that very object itself. Anyone who has tried to deal with two children quarrelling over a toy will recognize the situation. René Girard takes the process further: in order to possess the desired object, the rival must be eliminated. Once eliminated, though, the rival is no longer there to serve as a role model. The way out of the quandary is to idealize and revere the vanquished rival as a God, the ultimate role model.

The triangle composed of oneself, the desired object, and the model who is a rival because he possesses it, is a root cause of violence. The violence awakens whenever a person desires what another person desires because that person desires it. There is more than a parallel between what the New Testament teaches about violence on the one hand and about giving on the other: it is one and the same argument.

This kind of mimetic behaviour, including for instance the urge to keep up with the Joneses, thus generates deeprooted and pervasive violence in society. It is aggravated by its counterpart, the urge of the Joneses to preserve their lead, which transforms the process into an interminable chase.

Conformity without envy requires that we master our own desires. It is not just a matter of resisting extravagance and consumerism, or even of setting a bad example; it is more a matter of escaping the mechanisms whereby the satisfaction of one's one desires generate "trouble and cost for our neighbour,"[13] even if it be through long chains of causation.

An Inclusive Economy

Once some members of a society accept the idea that they can do without some of the others, they can entertain the prospect of destroying their neighbour in order to attract his or her goods to themselves.[14] War becomes an option. The essential cement of a peaceable economy is the shared desire of all its members to be part of a single society. "Here we have a prospect of one common interest from which our own is inseparable—that to turn all the treasures we possess into the channel of universal love becomes the business of our lives."[15]

Trustworthy economic agents

In a peaceable economy, economic agents, be they people or institutions, do not strive to deceive. They may none the less disappoint. "Do not put your trust in princes, in mortals, in whom there is no help. When their breath departs, they return to the earth; on that very day their plans perish" (Ps. 146:3-4). That is an inescapable limitation of the human condition, but the trustworthy do not seek intentionally to mislead.

Trust is indispensable to any economy. There are too many things going on to be constantly checking all of them. Without trust, the division of labour would be impossible. Society depends on trusting people to do what is expected of them. As the saying goes, "If everyone does his own job, the cows will be well looked after."[16] Trust is one of the ligaments holding the body of a community together: [T]he whole body, joined and held together by every supporting ligament, grows and builds itself up in love, as each part does its work." (Eph. 4:16).

If trust is to serve the peaceable economy, trustworthiness must go further than mere predictability or routinely sticking to rules. Deeper than that, it depends on empathy for the person or people whose trust is solicited. The aim is to reassure them that their needs are understood and to respond with compassion to the concerns of all parties involved—to the whole community of neighbours. Trustworthiness is an expression of neighbourly love, just as trust feeds neighbourly love.

Trust grows as people or institutions prove by experience that they can be trusted, that they are trustworthy. Trust often involves warm feelings. In so far as trust proves justified, the truster warms to the trusted. By the same token, the trusted warms to those who trust them. Feelings of friendship grow and trust gains in strength. Thus trust is one of the cumulative processes described in Chap. 2, as is of course its converse, distrust.

What with deception and disappointment, trustworthiness in particular is as demanding as loving one's neighbour. So much so that Jacques Ellul, one of the few Protestant theologians to have tackled the issue of trust, takes the view that it is an extreme expression of the unconditional love of our neighbour to which we are called.[17] Fortunately however, such pessimism seems far from social reality; by and large, people do trust each other. They do put themselves in each other's hands, accepting to depend on each other, often hardly thinking about it.

Win-Win, and Win

Photo: by Ed. Dommen

The photograph above illustrates the market ideal. The buyer is happy to have more carrots and less money; the seller is happy to have more money and fewer carrots. The community is happy because the transaction has generated revenues for the public benefit: rent to the municipality for the market stall, value-added tax to the state. Everyone has grounds to be happy, provided the gains are fairly shared among all the many parties directly or indirectly involved.

If the economy is to be free from frustration and the attendant feelings of injustice needing to be righted, then it must be composed exclusively of win-win transactions. There must be no loser longing for revenge. Losers are not necessarily worse off than they would have been if the transaction had not taken place; it may be that one or other of the participants feels that the gains of the operation have not been fairly distributed. In a peaceable economy, all parties involved not only feel that their share is fair, but they are confident that the others share the feeling. A peaceable outcome has a number of prerequisites. It requires being alert to the wishes of others, and before that the recognition that the others are worthy of consideration and that their wishes have as much weight as one's own. It requires an understanding of other people's feelings, and that in turn requires dialogue.

We have already seen that nearly all economic transactions involve three parties, not just two: the buyer, the seller, and the third parties—all the others who are affected by the transaction. Calvin was already aware of the importance of externalities, the effects of transactions on third parties: "[L] et us not consider only what is of advantage only to the individual with whom we have to deal, but consider also what is expedient for the public ... one must properly determine that the contract is of service to the community, rather than harmful."[18]

A transaction in which the winnings are shared between the buyer and the seller to the disregard or, worse still, to the detriment of third parties is not a peaceable outcome because an injustice has been done and a grudge has been sown.

Future generations are included among the third parties. Today's transactions must not impair their freedom to act as they choose.[19] That is the purport of the first sentence of the authoritative definition the World Commission on Environment and Development gave of "sustainable development": "Sustainable development is development that meets the needs of the present without compromising the ability of future generations to meet their own needs."[20] Otherwise, the prospect is as Wilfred Owen described it in his poem "Strange Meeting"[21]:

> Now men will go content with what we spoiled.
> Or, discontent, boil bloody, and be spilled.

Not to compromise the ability of future generations to meet their own needs is a demanding requirement. It needs modesty, a willingness to accept that future generations may choose needs for themselves which are not those which this generation would prefer to choose for them.

Friendly Rivalry

A peaceable economy surely enjoys some conflict. It is almost always essential in seeking an effective solution to a problem that is acceptable to all concerned. What distinguishes a peaceable economy is that the conflict is handled in a peaceable manner.

In some cases it is a matter of finding a single solution to a particular problem. A shared search for the right solution is the peaceable approach, not a struggle to vanquish the proposals of others in order to impose one's own already-decided solution.

In other cases conflict is an enduring feature of an activity. In the economy, competition is the prime example. Firms compete with each other for customers, either by offering a cheaper good, one of better quality, or a new good or service that meets a particular need more effectively.

When labour is in short supply, employers compete for it with each other by offering better pay or conditions, or a more interesting job. For this happy form of competition between employers to exist, labour must effectively be in short supply. That may be a matter of overall full employment, which is achieved by macroeconomic policy. This is beyond the control of any single employer.

If it is a matter of a particular type of labour—engineers, mathematicians, or whatever—supply depends to a significant degree on the availability of appropriate education and training. Along with competing with each other, the employers share an interest in ensuring that an adequate overall supply is trained. This is one of many situations in the economy where competition and cooperation work hand in hand.

Although a peaceable economy eschews enmity, it thrives on rivalry—provided it is friendly. The parallel with games is appropriate. Games often involve rivals sparring against each other. Each rival needs the others to spur it to give its best.

The World Trade Organization prides itself on providing appropriate conditions for playing games: the mission statement by its director-general on its website begins "WTO provides a forum for negotiating agreements aimed at reducing obstacles to international trade and ensuring *a level playing field* for all."[22] Oddly enough, it uses that phrase only in the English version of the statement. The other language versions talk of "equal conditions for everyone." Equal conditions and a level playing field are not only different matters, but independent of each other. Both are desirable, provided they are properly circumscribed.

In a game, rivalry can be intense; the game can engage each player's keenest efforts. But all play in the awareness that the opponents are an integral part of a single game. In that sense, all the players taken together form a single team, each member playing its own distinctive role in the overall scheme. The game takes place against a background of a common shared interest.

Another distinctive feature of games is that one can decide whether or not to play at all, and one can leave the game. One of the characteristics of a playing field (whether level or not) is that it has clearly marked boundaries. The game is played only within them. Unlike real life, games are not all-encompassing.

If one merges WTO's different language perspectives, one conjures up an image of a game between relatively equal opponents. Games are, however, often played between unequal opponents. If the game is to be fair when the players are unequal, some form of handicap system is needed. If the better players don't want to discourage their weaker opponents, then apart from the rules they need above all a considerate style of playing that ensures the weaker players enjoy the game. Otherwise they will not want to play—and remember that, as it is a game, they are free not to.

What if the matter at stake is too serious to be treated as a game, what if it is a question of life or death? People whose existence is at stake cannot sensibly be asked to behave in a spirit of shared pleasure as if they were playing a game. It is not a game, because they do not have the option of leaving it. In these conditions, they are likely to defend their existential interests by any means available, paying no more attention to the rules than is prudent and violating them if it can help to save their skins.

The commandment not to steal is no more than a rule of the game. The catechism of the Catholic Church draws the bounds of the playing field with respect to it: "There is no theft … if refusal is contrary to reason and the universal destination of goods. This is the case in obvious and urgent necessity when the only way to provide for immediate, essential needs (food, shelter, clothing . . .) is to put at one's disposal and use the property of others."[23]

It is up to the stronger party to treat people in such straits in all earnestness with special consideration.

> Let us look properly into the matter to see if we would like to be treated in the same way if we were in the place of the person who is growing weak and has nothing else with which to feed himself. We would be wanting others to act kindly towards us and support us.[24]

This is no more than an application of the Golden Rule,[25] "Do as you would be done by," which is a constant of all the great moral codes of humanity.[26] Here Calvin explicitly stresses the important point that we should treat others as we would like to be treated, not in the place where we ourselves are, but if we were in their place. The peaceable economy calls for empathy, for a willingness to make the effort to understand both the circumstances and the wishes of the other: that is what looking properly into the matter involves. The word "support" emphasizes the point because in French it has the double meaning of "to support" and "to put up with." We are called to act kindly even towards those who are not particularly likeable.

We have described the ubiquity of cumulative effects in the economy. A handicap system includes arranging before the start of play compensation for those who will be victims of the cumulative processes that generate deprivation. This relieves the weaker party of the pressure of need so that they can enter into the contest in the spirit of a game. Furthermore, the handicap must be granted freely and unconditionally. If any sense of obligation were aroused in the beneficiary, it would queer the game.

Basic income provides a simple but far-reaching device serving the double objective in question here. The proposal is that everyone should receive an unconditional basic income, identical for all, on the simple, single ground that they exist. Firstly, it would constantly redistribute income towards the marginalized; secondly, it would by the same token provide the base on which everyone could participate in the economy free of the pressures of urgent need and thus in the spirit of a game. In this way, it meets some of the essential prerequisites of a peaceable economy. The idea is more than utopian, since schemes approximating it function in some places and pilot projects have recently been conducted in others.[26]

It Is the Spirit Which Is Decisive

Peaceable economies are compatible with a wide range of forms of economic organization. Outcrops of peaceable economy can appear in virtually any economy. Conversely, even picturesque local varieties of economy beloved of anthropologists can take oppressive forms either in their internal organization or at least by the exclusion which their frontiers establish. It is not the structure of the economy that determines its peaceable nature, but the spirit in which it functions.

The Last Word

A peaceable economy embodies *shalom*. It is a magnificently complex concept, involving not just peace, but harmony, completeness, or wholeness, physical and spiritual. In the same sense as "The kingdom of God is among you", shalom can thrive between the contestants in a demanding contest. They form a single whole in their contest. "Peace, peace, to the far and the near, says the Lord" (Is. 57:19). Shalom is called in one breath upon those that are far off and those that are near, both together. Here we are in the economy of externalities, of backwash and spread effects. It is not good enough to content only those who are close to us, whatever be the sense of 'close'.

"For the whole law is summed up in a single commandment, 'You shall love your neighbor as yourself'" (Gal. 5:14). In describing the conditions required to achieve a peaceable economy—and their converse, the conditions that correspond to a warlike economy—we have done no more than spell out the implications of this pithy statement. We have not even tried to explore its implications exhaustively, but we have explored them sufficiently to realize how far-reaching they are. Just to comprehend their extent is demanding. To fulfil the law, even though it is so simple to state, is extremely demanding.

A Parenthesis: To Be at Peace with Oneself

> Imitate the action of the swan
> Peaceful on the surface
> Paddling like hell underneath
> – Sign hanging in the office of the government
>   economist in Kiribati a few years ago.

To be at peace with oneself, to enjoy inner peace, is a nice feeling. However, it has little to do with the peaceable economy, because the peaceable economy has everything to do with one's neighbour.

In an economic perspective, to be in a state of inner peace involves being satisfied both with what one has and with what one does, with what one takes and what one makes. The gap between such satisfaction and self-satisfaction is tiny. Although one may be satisfied with what one has, it does not follow that others share one's opinion.

People may have too much. It is not just that they may set a greedy standard for themselves; it may be that the economic system in its general functioning may have shunted more than their share in their direction. We must be alert to how we have come by what we have, and whether some of it may not be due to others, if we are to avoid committing theft in the sense of the sixth commandment.

People may, on the other hand, be using too little, letting a part of their possessions go to waste when these could serve to provide a livelihood or goods of which the poor are thereby deprived. "To renounce riches is not in itself virtuous, but rather a vain ambition … Love is the bond of perfection, and those who deprive others along with themselves of the use of money deserve no praise."[27] Note that in French, as in English, the word "vain" has two meanings, both of which apply here: first, as serving vanity, and second as futile in that it is ineffective in achieving its aim, as we shall explain below.

John Woolman, who seems to have swallowed Calvin whole, spelled out much the same idea: "People who have large possessions and live in the spirit of charity, who carefully inspect the circumstance of those who occupy their estates, and regardless of the customs of the times regulate their demands agreeable to universal love—these ... do good to the poor without placing it as an act of bounty."[28]

People whose lifestyle leaves them at peace with themselves may feel that they are setting an example for others. Maybe they are, but they should beware of overestimating their influence. Being a role model is all the more effective if it is carefully staged. It was said that it cost a fortune to keep Gandhi in poverty.[29] John Woolman ostentatiously wore undyed clothes because they were an easily noticed sign of an alternative lifestyle, free from the "unquiet spirit in which wars are generally carried on."[30] In the gospels, the Evangelists are very careful how they set the stage for Jesus' prophetic acts.

Greed—which those whose lifestyle leaves them in inner peace claim to be free from—is one of the seven traditional deadly sins, but so is the pride into which their choice may draw them.

To be at peace with ourselves in our lifestyle is not just a matter of what we have or choose to forgo, it is equally a matter of what we do. Are we devoting enough of our time and talents to the common good? Commenting on the parable of the talents, Calvin explains that "Christ simply means that there is no excuse for the lazy who suppress God's gifts and spend their lives in idleness."[31] Sloth is also one of the deadly sins.

Devoting our time and talents to the common good is not necessarily the same thing as working as defined by the ILO: that is, working for pay or profit. On the one hand, not all work thus defined serves the common good, and on the other hand there is a wide range of unpaid or unprofitable activities that do serve the common good. "Whoever helps human society and brings profit to it through their industry, whether in managing their family or administering public or private affairs, or advising or teaching others, or by any other means whatsoever, cannot be counted among the idle."[32]

There is a form of escape from the social realities of the economy that resembles a similarly escapist form of pacifism. There are pacifists who do not want to dirty their hands by participating in bloody conflict but who do nothing to try and obviate the conflict itself. It is possible to piggyback on the economy, but impossible to withdraw from it.

Whether we like it or not, we are part of one another.

Part Two

Finding a Peaceable Economy

6. Models of Ideal Economy

Ever since David Hume's *Treatise on Human Nature* (which bears the subtitle *Being an Attempt to Introduce the Experimental Method of Reasoning into Moral Subjects*), published in 1739, the distinction between "is" and "ought" has become fundamental in Anglo-Saxon philosophy. Statements using "is" describe the way things are, the nature of reality. Their validity is open to scrutiny according to scientific method. "Ought" statements pass judgement. Things, behaviour, etc. are assessed according to standards that may be moral or, more generally, related to any kind of goal. Thus, a poisoner whose victim has not died might say, "I ought to have used more poison."[1]

We have seen however that reality is so complicated that it can only be comprehended if it is described in terms of some kind of model. From a model that purports to describe reality to one that describes an ideal state is a small step. Above all, the language used in both cases is the same, and it is "is" language. How then does one distinguish between the two kinds of model? Economics provides a case in point. The neo-liberal model that is currently dominant as a purported description of economic reality in fact describes an ideal state.

Apart from comparing the realism of two models by seeing which stands up better to testing against reality, one can examine their assumptions. In models of ideal states, some at least are patently unrealistic once they are fully spelled out. Have you ever met a *homo œconomicus*?

Confronted with a model of society that doesn't correspond to reality, there are two options. One is to change the assumptions of the model to bring them closer to reality. The other is to work to change behaviour in the hopes of bringing it closer to the requirements of the model. If we choose the latter course, we may be assuming that the model describes a state of affairs more desirable than the current one. Alternatively, we may be so wedded to a given model in our way of apprehending the world or simply of earning our living that we refuse to revise it. It is worth reflecting which of these two possibilities applies to present-day economics or to any particular economist.

To promote particular behavioural ideals is a traditional function of many religions. They have toolkits of techniques for this purpose, sermons being one verbal example among many. They constitute classic examples of "ought"-discourse. Non-verbal means of influencing the behaviour of others can also be included in the toolkit, like the force of example. As the Quakers say, "Let your lives speak." The phrase can be traced back to George Fox (1624–1691), one of the founders of the Quaker movement. He actually wrote, "Let your lives preach," which underlines the religious context of the advice.[2]

Utopias

A utopia is an ideal construct describing a desirable state of affairs. Once it has been elaborated, its prerequisites can be analyzed to see whether it could be achieved in the real world—whether behaviour could be brought into line with the requirements of the model.

A double etymology can be attributed to the word "utopia," both from Greek roots. On the one hand, it may come from eu-topia, a perfect place; on the other, it may be u-topia, nowhere. The term was invented by Thomas More (1447/8[3]–1535) in his book *Utopia*, published in Latin in 1516. Its subtitle, *The Best State of a Republic, and of the New Island Utopia*, captures both senses in the "Best State" and the "New Island" respectively.

Utopias are located nowhere in space. They are often portrayed as being on an island to stress their separation from the rest of, or the real, world (Islands often have a dream quality for people who live on continents). Otherwise utopias may be located in some place purporting to be real but far away, so that they can be romanticized with little risk of contradiction, like the Stone Age economies of Marshall Sahlins.[4]

Utopias are none the less always rooted in the culture from which they spring, because their intention is to describe how things could or should be, compared to a real and particular imperfect state that is familiar to the public concerned. They always imply an incitement to move from where we are towards this better situation. In other words, though they are described in "is"-language, they fall into the "ought" category. The description of Agathotopia by James Meade clearly describes these characteristics and functions of utopias, including an explicit reference to the real society with which Agathotopia is being compared.

As to the characteristics of this Agathotopia, note the inclusion of the dynamics of cumulative causation in the last two paragraphs. We shall return on occasion to Meade's model utopia as our argument unfolds.

Agathotopia[5]

I recently set sail to visit the island of Utopia which, I have been told, constitutes a Perfect Place to live in. But, alas, I could find the island Nowhere. However on my way home I chanced to visit the nearby island of Agathotopia. The inhabitants made no claim for perfection in their social arrangements, but they did claim the island to be a Good place to live in. I studied their institutions closely, came to the conclusion that their social arrangements were indeed about as good as one could hope to achieve in this wicked world, and returned home to recommend Agathotopian arrangements for my own country.

I am making Agathotopian rather than Utopian recommendations simply because I could not find Utopia. But the reason why I could not find that island was something of a mystery. The Agathotopians seemed to have no basically hostile feelings towards their Utopian neighbours, but were very secretive about them and strangely unwilling to help me to find the island. I was very puzzled until some remarks by the rather decrepit Agathotopian economist Professor Dr Semaj Edaem ["James Meade" backwards; he was more than 80 years old when he wrote this book] inadvertently suggested to me the following explanation of their reserved attitude to the Utopians.

The Utopians have, I suspect, gone in for genetic engineering in a big way and have produced a race of perfect human beings. The Agathotopians are in many ways a conservative lot and have been either unable or, as I suspect, unwilling to follow Plato in taking the necessary measures to breed genetically a race of people with inborn perfect social behaviour. The Utopians, if I am right, have the task of producing perfect institutions for perfect human beings; the Agathotopians have tried only to produce good institutions for imperfect people.

If this is the explanation of the Agathotopian attitude towards the utopians my study of Agathotopia suggests a very important connection between institutions and behaviour. The Agathotopians have devised institutions which rely very largely on self-centred enterprising behaviour in a free competitive market but which, at the same time, put great stress upon cooperation between individuals in producing the best possible outcome and upon a compassionate attitude to those who would otherwise lose out. The typical Agathotopian has a more cooperative and compassionate attitude in his or her social behaviour than is the case at present in the United Kingdom, where we have, alas, been subject for so many years to such a regime of devil-take-the-hindmost and grab-as-much-money-as-quickly-as-possible. This suggests that there is some positive feedback between social institutions and social attitudes.

If this interpretation is true, it means that it will be difficult at first for us to enjoy the advantages of Agathotopian institutions until there has been time for the positive feedbacks between institutions and attitudes to operate effectively. But there is also the implication that it may not be a waste of time to make Agathotopian institutional changes which are somewhat out of harmony with present attitudes, but may well in time help to mould these attitudes in the desired direction.

Golden Ages: The Economy of Paradise

There is no requirement regarding the location of utopias in time. They are sometimes located in the author's present, like James Meade's Agathotopia. Golden ages are utopias usually located in the past. Some cultures insert a golden age into a recurring cycle of ages. Paradise before the fall can be, and has been, taken as a golden age.

It is hardly surprising that Calvin, the reformer who devoted the most thought to economic questions, had a view on the nature of the economy in Paradise before the fall. The starting point, in the most literal sense, is God's boundless generosity. Everything is a gift of God. "In the very order of the creation the paternal solicitude of God for man is conspicuous, because he furnished the world with all things needful, and even with an immense profusion of wealth, before he formed man. Thus man was rich before he was born."[6] The economy of Paradise was thus one of abundance. "No corner of the earth was then barren, nor was there even any which was not exceedingly rich and fertile: ... not only was there an abundant supply of food, but with it was added sweetness for the gratification of the palate, and beauty to feast the eyes."[7]

There was work in Paradise. Adam delved and Eve span, as the English priest John Ball had already said in the 14th century. Calvin expands: "Moses now adds, that the earth was given to humanity on this condition, that they should occupy themselves in its cultivation. Whence it follows that people were created to employ themselves in some activity, and not to lay about in inactivity and idleness. This labour, on the other hand was pleasant, and full of delight, far from any trouble and weariness."[8]

From the outset, God intended humans to be sociable. Although Paradise had only two inhabitants at the fall, they were the spring of society. "Now Moses explains God's design in creating woman. It is that there should be people on the earth, conversing with each other [or supporting each other[9]] in mutual sociability. The basic starting point is therefore that God created humans to be sociable creatures."[10]

Adam delved and Eve span: God gave different gifts to different people, so they need to exchange with each other.[11] Calvin proceeds directly from there to an economic image.

> Those who put to good use whatever gifts God has given them are said to be engaged in trading. The life of the faithful is justly compared to trading, for they have to exchange and barter with each other in order to keep the community together. Indeed the industry with which each person discharges the office assigned him, the calling itself, the dexterity with which he carries it out, and other gifts, are reckoned to be so many kinds of merchandise; because the use or objective which they have in view is to promote natural intercourse among people.[12]

Paradise not only had an economy, it was a sophisticated one. Here is a pointer to the economy of the Kingdom of God.

States of Nature

The "state of nature" is yet another matter. It is no more intended to describe an ideal than a reality. It is intended as a benchmark against which reality can be assessed. It is a conceptual tool.

It may be far from paradisiac. For Thomas Hobbes (1588–1679) the state of nature refers to the natural tendencies of humans when they are not restrained by "a common power to keep them all in awe." In the absence of such a power, human life is

> solitary, poor, nasty, brutish, and short. [I]n the nature of man, we find three principal causes of quarrel. First, competition; secondly, diffidence [in its etymological meaning of distrust]; thirdly, glory. The first maketh men invade for gain; the second, for safety; and the third, for reputation. The first use violence, to make themselves masters of other men's persons, wives, children, and cattle; the second, to defend them; the third, for trifles, as a word, a smile, a different opinion, and any other sign of undervalue.

This state is not necessarily related to any particular period in the evolution of humanity.[13]

For David Hume (1711–1776), the state of nature is simply a philosophical device: "philosophers may, if they please, extend their reasoning to the suppos'd state of nature; provided they allow it to be a mere philosophical fiction, which never had, and never cou'd have any reality."[14] In any event, for Hume, as for Hobbes, the state of nature holds no particular attraction: "This state of nature, therefore, is to be regarded as a mere fiction, not unlike that of the golden age, which poets have invented; only with this differ-ence, that the former is describ'd as full of war, violence and injustice; whereas the latter is painted out to us, as the most charming and most peaceable condition, that can possibly be imagin'd."[15]

Jean-Jacques Rousseau (1712–1778) probably helped spread the idea that the state of nature must be desirable—with the assistance of Voltaire's witticism about his descrip-tion of it: "When one reads your work, one is taken with the desire to walk on all fours."[16] It is certainly true that Rous-seau takes issue with Hobbes; life in the state of nature is not nasty, brutish, or even particularly short. There is plenty of work and therefore of healthy exercise. It also true accord-ing to Rousseau that the current state of actual society is an unhappy one. Rousseau's state of nature is not sociable. Indeed, it is explicitly a conceptual construct designed to isolate the characteristics of humanity in the absence of society. Like Hume, he says that it is a "state which exists no longer, maybe never existed and probably never will, but which is none the less necessary … to judge our present state."[17] In the absence of social relations, and therefore of language, humans lack the conceptual tools and the very desire to ask themselves whether they are miserable. There can be no moral categories like good or evil because morality is a social phenomenon.

Even in these conditions however, Rousseau imbues humans with one social characteristic: inborn sympathy for others. The natural instinct for self-preservation encouraged them not to fight each other since combat was not necessary to survival, and sympathy—repulsion at the suffering of others—held them back from useless combat.[18]

Since lasting social relations must be excluded from Rousseau's state of nature, there must be plenty of room for everyone so that they are not constantly meeting each other. Indeed it is when space runs short that society and trouble both begin. "The first person who, having enclosed a field, had the idea of saying 'This is mine' and found people silly enough to believe him, was the real founder of civil society. What crimes, wars, murders, misery and horrors would have been spared to humankind if someone had pulled out the fenceposts or filled in the ditch, crying 'Beware of listening to this impostor.'"[19]

Hobbes, Hume, and Rousseau are but three examples of the legion of writers who have resorted to the device of states of nature. Daniel Defoe's novel *Robinson Crusoe* embroiders on the image.[20] Robinson Crusoe personifies the state of nature in a family of economic models that start from a single economic agent who is both the sole producer and the sole consumer. He decides in sovereign solitude how to allocate the time and other resources at his disposal to best meet his needs and desires. This is handy for economists who want to promote the image of the economy as based on isolated individuals free from any social concern.

On the other hand, in the novel a second person, Friday, turns up on the island, and Robinson Crusoe immediately makes him his servant. As the joke goes, "The only person who ever got all his work done by Friday is Robinson Crusoe." Thus, relations of subordination and exploitation appear at the same time as society, not to mention contempt: Robinson Crusoe makes no attempt to discover his new companion's name. "I made him know his Name should be Friday…; I likewise taught him to say Master."[21]

The Kingdom of God

> What the Bible calls the kingdom of God represents
> the horizon of expectation of the world.
> – Henry Mottu[22]

The economy of the kingdom of God is surely peaceable. If we can locate the kingdom, we shall have located the peaceable economy. The problem is that there is no agreement on its location, but a wide range of hypotheses.

Henry Mottu's comment quoted above encapsulates all its uncertainties while preserving all its richness. It recalls a Soviet joke. The apocryphal Radio Erevan is said to have had a phone-in programme. A listener phones in: "When will communist society come?" The commentator answers "Communism is on the horizon, and we are advancing towards it." Later another listener phones in: "What is the horizon?" Reply: "It is the line where heaven and earth join; it recedes as one advances toward it."

The kingdom of God is posited as a longed-for, desirable state that we hope to achieve. For many, it will come at the end of time, perhaps even following cataclysmic events that may wipe out the very memory of what went before. For others, creation can progress towards the radiant objective just as Marx's historical materialism ultimately culminates in the communist society. Yet others hold that the kingdom of God cannot materialize in this world; it is in a different realm. It would be fruitless to explore, not to mention evaluate, all the ramifications of the debate. Visions of the future are dizzying in their multitude of tangled perspectives. The range of views originating within any single tradition or absorbed into it from outside sources like classical Greek philosophy for Christians already make the mind boggle.

Suffice it for present purposes to focus on the terse phrase in Luke 17:21: "the kingdom of God is within you." The kingdom of God is therefore already here, in each one of us. If we only opened ourselves to it and cultivated it, it could blossom in the here and now. The Greek phrase thus translated in the King James Version can equally be translated "the kingdom of God is *among* you" and several English translations of the Bible use that form.[23] In that version the kingdom is no less present in the here and now, but rather than being tucked away inside individuals, it lies in the midst of the community. It recalls Matthew 18:20, "For where two or three are gathered in my name, I am there among them." As Calvin puts it, "It is as if one said that the saints are gathered into the society of Christ on the principle that they should share with one another all the gifts which God confers upon them. This does not, however rule out the diversity of graces."[24] Indeed the fact that God gives different talents to different people explains the need for several people to be assembled together to realize the community that is the kingdom. The kingdom is present, but it may be difficult to discern. "For now we see in a mirror, dimly . . . Now I know only in part" (1 Cor. 13:12). But we can work to clear away the rubbish; then the kingdom can be realized.

Leonhard Ragaz (1868–1945) describes the steps which need to be taken: "respect for the right [sic] of humanity, especially of the weak and the poor; condemnation of the idols of Mammon and violence, protest in the name of God against devaluing, degrading, enslaving and profaning humanity, as well as against the whole of any world which rests on such iniquities."[25] It is not enough just to take them, however; they need to be followed by effect.

7. Can We Get There from Here?

The Invisible Hand

As every individual, therefore, endeavours as much as he can … to direct [his] industry that its produce maybe of the greatest value; every individual necessarily labours to render the annual revenue of the society as great as he can. He generally, indeed, neither intends to promote the public interest, nor knows how much he is promoting it … He intends only his own security; and by directing that industry in such a manner as its produce may be of the greatest value, he intends only his own gain; and he is in this, as in many other cases, led by an invisible hand to promote an end which was no part of his intention. Nor is it always the worse for the society that it was no part of it. By pursuing his own interest, he frequently promotes that of the society more effectually than when he really intends to promote it. I have never known much good done by those who affected to trade for the public good. It is an affectation, indeed, not very common among merchants, and very few words need be employed in dissuading them from it.[1]

Adam Smith's model of an invisible hand is at the root of laisser-faire economics and its avatars, including today's neo-liberalism. This concept, which has so firmly established his fame, did not actually play the central role in his own scheme of things that it acquired later on. In any event, the drawback of this happy ideal is its lack of realism. It ignores several inescapable features of any economy.

It assumes that there are no externalities—that no transaction between two parties has any side effect on unwilling or unwitting third parties. Calvin, two centuries earlier, was less readily convinced: "Let us not consider only what is of advantage only to the individual with whom we have to deal, but consider also what is expedient for the public. For … one must properly determine that the contract is of service generally, rather than harmful."[2] Secondly, it assumes that the transaction is an isolated event that is not part of any general dynamic process such as described in Chap. 2. Thirdly, it assumes that the buyer and seller are reasonably equal in bargaining power so that each gets a fair share of the benefits of the transaction. Indeed, it ignores the possibility of oppression or outright theft such that one party to the transaction gains by taking away some of the other party's substance.

Inequality includes inequality in information. Acquiring information involves costs; the rich therefore have better access to it. Worse still, one party to a transaction can wilfully exploit the credulity or ignorance of the other. The importance of unequal access to information was underlined by the 2010 Nobel Prize in Economics, awarded to three economists for their work on it. In his award speech, the chairman of the Economics Sciences Prize Committee illustrated the social significance of their work:

> They have also shown that resource utilisation in a search market is generally not socially efficient, since there are indirect effects that individual agents do not take into account. If one unemployed person increases her own search activity, it will become more difficult for other job seekers to find employment. At the same time, it will be easier for a recruiting firm to fill its vacancies.[3]

Economic War

It is precisely the awareness of unequal bargaining power and its resulting exploitation that led to the idea of class war so central to Marxist thought. The exploited classes are encouraged in this model to join forces to retaliate in violent conflict with the rich and powerful who are exploiting them. In Marxism this was taken up by the industrial proletariat, in Maoism by the peasantry. Well before all that, class war had broken out in peasant uprisings such as the peasants' war of 1524–1525 in Germany, in which Thomas Müntzer parted company with Luther. Roughly speaking, Luther was defending authority and order, while Müntzer was fighting for more fairness.[4] Colonial wars were also a resort to violence by rich and powerful interests to wrest control over wealth and resources from weaker adversaries.

Either side can take the initiative in class war. As the US billionaire Warren Buffett famously said, "There's class warfare all right, but it's my class, the rich class, that's making war, and we're winning."[5] And even in the absence of intention, the dynamics through which prosperity and deprivation feed on each other contain intrinsic violence. The rich have a longer life expectancy than the poor. Thus structural violence is built willy-nilly into the very foundations of any economy.

During the "thirty glorious years" of prosperity underpinned by social democracy—from the end of World War II to the 1970s in the developed market economies—income and wealth were relatively well-distributed in Europe and to some extent elsewhere while prosperity grew and was shared. But this was also the period of the Cold War. The powerful in the West, afraid that the alternative model centred on the Soviet Union would seduce their own people, went to great lengths to head off the frustrations and demands of their own underclasses. Cold War turned out to be a substitute for class war, with the threat of violence always lurking in the wings.

That ended with the fall of the Berlin wall. Since then, income inequality has resumed its secular growth while the economic growth that neo-liberals believe to spring naturally from a liberal economy has tailed off in the countries that benefited from the thirty glorious years. As a Soviet official in the United Nations said at the time, "The socialist system was very beneficial for the working classes—in the West."[6]

Homo Œconomicus

The economist Amartya Sen (who won the Nobel prize in economics in 1998) sketches a delightful vignette of economic man, *homo œconomicus*. "Two *homines œconomici* meet: 'Where is the railway station?' he asks me. 'There,' I say, pointing at the post office, 'and would you please post this letter for me on the way?' 'Yes,' he says, determined to open the envelope and check whether it contains something valuable.'"[7]

Each is pursuing his or her own interest exclusively, treating the other as a mere instrument, totally lacking in any sense of lasting social relationships cemented by honesty or trust. *Homo œconomicus* is a caricature. "As the greatest economic philosophers … have all recognized, *homo œconomicus*, the acquisitive, emotionally cardboard, and socially atomistic construct of academic economics is a reductio ad absurdum."[8]

One would indeed have great difficulty in finding any professional economist who maintains that *homo œconomicus* corresponds to any sort of real person. It is a theoretical construct, an assembly of assumptions designed to support theoretical models of the economy. The trouble is that some economists, and more politicians and business executives, take the models for pictures of reality. Indeed they strive to construct a reality that conforms to the model, treating it not just as a simplified picture of reality but as an ideal to be achieved.

The Biblical Ideal

The Bible paints a clear picture of a very different ideal person, who "requires a heart so admirably arranged as not to be prompted in the slightest degree contrary to the law of love" (Calvin box §50). Such persons love their neighbour like themselves, no matter where their neighbour may be located on the globe and regardless of how uncongenial the neighbour might be. The ideal person of the Bible is particularly solicitous of the poor, the weak and the defenceless. The ideal is thus portrayed, circumstantially and emphatically, in Matthew 25:31-46.

The characteristics of the biblically ideal person are essential to a peaceable economy. Nor is it enough that a few people embody them. They must characterize society as a whole if the entire society is to be peaceable.

This ideal person is the stuff of countless sermons because he or she so clearly falls into the "ought" category rather than the "is." However, notwithstanding centuries—nay, millennia—of teaching and preaching, humanity does not seem to have moved noticeably closer to the ideal. Maybe the good news is that it has not moved noticeably further away from it either. In any event, there is little evidence of moral progress in humanity in general. That is not deny that history has known—and rightly admires—people who have come markedly closer the ideal than others.

There have been energetic efforts to cultivate a new human. The twentieth-century socialist system worked hard at it, especially through education and the channelling of social relations (It should, incidentally be remembered that the social ideals of socialism resembled the biblical ideal in many essentials.). Yet socialist morality was no more effective in taking root in socialist society than any other morality elsewhere. Nor, on the hand, was it noticeably less effective.

Eric Gill's bas-relief outside the Council Chamber of Geneva's Palais des Nations was Britain's gift to the nascent League of Nations. The League was soon to die an early death: the bas-relief was installed in 1938 when the storm of the second world war was already gathering. It intentionally imitates Michelangelo's painting on the ceiling of the Sistine Chapel, *The Creation of Adam*. A memorandum of 1935 describing Eric Gill's design states, "the central panel represents the *re*-creation of man, which the League of Nations is assisting."[9] There are, however, significant differences between the two representations. In Gill's version, the hand of Man (who is not just Adam) is not lifeless, waiting for the vivifying touch of the creator; it is outstretched towards God, upturned like a beggar's. And God's hand is not reaching down from above as the overall perspective of the Sistine original implies, but reaching out as a helping hand.

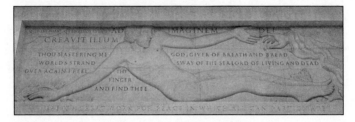

Figure 1. Eric Gill, bas-relief, Palais de Nations, Geneva.

8. Alternatives to Violence

Taking the example of armed conflict as a starting point, conscientious objection can take either of two forms. On the one hand, objectors can turn their back on the conflict, refusing to take part in it themselves. On the other hand, objectors can strive to bring about a peaceful settlement, or even defuse the situation before it turns into violent conflict. Non-objectors can also do this, and they often do. The Nobel Peace Prize is often awarded to pairs of belligerents who have reached a settlement.

Other variations exist. Objectors can actively support one side in an armed conflict against the other while refusing to carry arms. Objectors of this kind engage in unarmed branches of the war effort, such as the ambulance service.

Alternative Economics

Throughout history and against the background of many kinds of economy, there have been objectors of similar kinds.

There have been hermits or others who withdraw from the ambient economy. Some do not actually quit the economy but live as parasites upon it, for example by begging. Calvin, a master of invective, reserved some of his most virulent remarks for monks, whom he placed in that category: "For they are quite happy that everyone should undress themselves to clothe them; they don't know what it is to give something to others. That is why I usually call them "doctors of passive charity," in that they let people do as much good for them as they can."[1] There have always been countless experiments with utopian communities who strive to live a more just or less exploitative life outside or on the fringes of the ambient economy. It would be invidious to give specific present-day examples because there are so many. Some of them clamour for attention on Internet; others keep their head down and get on with the job of earning a livelihood. They may be firmly rooted in the peculiarities of their local culture and environment. They may not be suitable as models for a world economy to rival or replace the current one, but they express the diversity of graces.

Maybe there is no need for a single global model of economy. A single model of society valid for everyone everywhere, not to mention for all time, is not only unattractive but—fortunately—likely to be unworkable. The story of Babel (Gen. 11:1-9) is a cautionary tale in that regard. Its punch line in verse 8 can be read as a message of hope: "So the Lord scattered them abroad from there over the face of all the earth, and they left off building the city." They were scattered, they developed a variety of cultures, they turned to building a variety of smaller communities. Does it follow that E. F. Schumacher was right, that small is beautiful?[2] Diversity is a source of resilience. Small-scale social experiments allow innovations to be tested before applying them on a larger scale. Diversity fosters fecundity. Economists, the discipline of economics, and above all the economies of the world would all gain from the range of discoveries to be made and shared.

Alternative schemes cannot escape fitting into the larger picture. A present-day Robin Crusoe would be no less affected by global warming than anyone else. There is no escape from engagement with the world.

Then there have been those who have tried to leaven the economy with more humane behaviour, by their own example or by campaigning for social reform. As individuals, Francis of Assisi or Gandhi spring to mind; people like them have had a lasting and widespread influence moderating the general rapacity of the economy. Social currents like the Quaker or other industrialists of the 19th and early 20th centuries have inspired efforts to humanize the market economy.[3]

Numerous pressure groups and non-governmental organizations are campaigning for a more decent and honest economy, or a less exploitative one. At a more official level, international institutions like the International Labour Organization bring together workers, employers, and governments to agree on international norms of decent labour relations.

Can Human Nature Change?

Human nature as it really exists is far more than the unattractively selective simplification of *homo œconomicus*, but far from the ideal that the Bible is constantly calling us to realize.

Is humanity capable of progressing towards the ideal? The very concept of progress has its advances and its reverses. It had its heyday in the 19th and early 20th century. It reached its highest point in the positivism of Auguste Comte (1798–1857) and above all in the historical determinism of Karl Marx (1818–1883). Progress was sometimes represented as a railway. The image came naturally because railways provided an impressive display of the technical and scientific prowess of the period (Figure 2).

A century earlier, the Geneva cartoonist Rodolphe Töpffer had presented a more balanced view of a railway as a vehicle of progress (Figure 3).

In any event, trains need no steering wheel. They progress along rails already laid towards a destination determined in advance. The only element that remains amenable to choice is the speed at which it advances. In Marxism, where progress involves resolving a succession of contradictions between theses and antitheses, the pace of advance is difficult to predict;

Figure 2. José-María Sert, *Technical Progress*, mural in the Council Chamber, Palais des Nations, Geneva, 1935–1936.

Figure 3.[4]

indeed, there can be reverses on the way. But in the end, the ultimate destination, the communist society, will be reached.

Progress can be subdivided into a number of categories, such as scientific, technical, social, or moral. The existence of scientific and technical progress is hardly contested provided one avoids passing judgement on its moral qualities. The atomic bomb of 1945 was undoubtedly a triumph for science, but equally certainly a moral nadir. Nor was such inventiveness necessary to reach it: the bombing of Dresden with conventional weapons earlier the same year was no less horrific. It is revealing that no one has written a Wikipedia article on moral progress.[5] There is no article at all on "progress" in the *Encyclopédie du protestantisme*. The very humanity of humans is more an aspiration than a fact, at least if we share Otfried Höffe's view of humanity as he expressed it in his *Lexikon der Ethik*:

> Literally, humanity signifies what distinguishes humans from other living beings: its nature or essence. Humanity also signifies humankind, that is, the whole constituted of the human beings of the past, present and future. Finally, as a qualitative noun, it signifies an attitude or act which is not unworthy of a human.
>
> Human nature does not lock people into predetermined forms of behaviour and life. They are open beings, disposing of an extraordinarily wide field of action within

which they can develop and act, as individuals or in large or restricted groups. One can then speak of humanisation, or accession to humanity, or realisation of human qualities which at the outset were only virtualities or dispositions. In this perspective, humanity cannot be reduced to a biological process; to be human is to "become human" by (self-) education and by freely giving meaning to the world and to history. 'Humanity' thus signifies neither an empirical state of affairs, nor a pre-established model, but a task which people have to define and accomplish in a process of learning, discovery and projection of oneself which is never completed … 'Humanity' is not so much the baseness, weakness and decay of a "human, all too human" humanity, but rather the normative guiding idea, valid for the personal, social and political life of a truly-human-being determined by human self-realisation and solidarity. [6]

There is no firm evidence that humanity has progressed in its human qualities over history. The odds are that humanity will continue to muddle on as before. Not only individuals but collectivities will continue to display both admirable and deplorable traits of character and forms of behaviour. Both, unfortunately, will continue to inspire others in their wake. Above all, people will forget. "Those who cannot remember the lessons of history are condemned to repeat them," to paraphrase George Santayana.[7] Each generation must learn the lessons of life over again for itself. That is indeed part of the freedom from predetermined forms of behaviour and life that Höffe extolls.

Meanwhile . . .

Here are a few approaches that can contribute towards making most kinds of economy more peaceable. They do little more than spell out the implications of *love your neighbour like yourself.*

Make sure everyone can enjoy the game.

First, everyone should be free to take part in the economy, free from the pressures of immediate need so that they can enjoy it as a game. Everyone's means of subsistence should therefore be assured. In the mainstream market economy, we can achieve this through an all-embracing system of social security. It could be achieved even more simply and thoroughly by an unconditional basic income. In other types of economy, different means are practised to ensure that everyone is provided for.

Second, everyone means everyone. There should be no exclusion. Anyone excluded or threatened with exclusion should be helped to join into an economy satisfactory to them. That may mean bringing them into the fold of the mainstream economy in the spirit of the parable of the lost sheep,[8] but it may equally involve leaving their own economy intact or supporting its efforts to make it more viable and inclusive.

Take everyone seriously.

Peaceable economies meet the needs of their own participants without compromising the ability of others to meet their own needs.[9] To understand their needs, it is essential to listen to them. As George Fox (1624–1691), the pioneer of Quakerism, put it, "walk cheerfully over the world, answering that of God in every one": answering, not bossing.

That involves respecting other economies elsewhere, but it no less involves respecting diverse approaches to economic activity at home. That cannot be achieved without participatory democracy or other ways of concerting the different interests present without oppressing or suppressing them.

One implication of taking everyone seriously is to cultivate win-win-win situations, outcomes where buyers, sellers,[10] and the rest of the community are all better off with an activity than they would be without it. That involves listening to all three categories of stakeholder in any issue. It involves being attentive to externalities—the costs and benefits that fall on third parties—in order to minimize the social costs and help the victims deal with them,[11] and exploit the social benefits to the fullest extent possible.

It also involves doing one's best to take into account the stakeholders who cannot speak for themselves, like the environment or future generations, while trying to avoid projecting one's own desires onto them.

Encourage collective goods & services.
As soon as such a good is available to anyone, it is by the same token available to everyone within reach (This limit is extremely important, and the first point above must be brought into play in order to deal with it.). Collective goods do not feed greed or emulation. There is no reason to fight for one's share, since the full amount is spontaneously available.

Collective goods should be made available as widely as possible. Whenever possible, it is preferable to provide services by means of collective goods rather than "rival" ones (i.e., ones that can be made available to one user only at the expense of others who are thereby deprived of it).

Everyone must pay their fair share of taxes.
Since the workings of more or less every kind of economy enrich the rich while impoverishing the poor, or those at the centre at the expense of those on the periphery, it is necessary to return to the marginalized that which has been sucked away from them. Since collective goods are freely available to everyone, the market cannot generate a price for them as it does for "rival" goods. A simple and reasonably fair solution is to make it available free of charge and to pay for it through taxation. For expenses like these, among others, collectivities

need to raise taxes. If discontent and oppression are to be avoided, everyone concerned needs to feel that they are fair. That is best achieved through the democratic and participatory determination of how they are raised as well as how they are spent. No member of the community should escape paying their fair share, which is not to say that the community may not agree that certain members should not be subject to particular taxes.

Taxes can be paid in cash or in kind. They can include labour services. The International Labour Organization (ILO) frowns on them because it associates them with forced labour. On the other hand, they are frequently contributed by happy participants in small-scale entities.

The best means of taxation are the ones that those who are contributing consider fairest, bearing in mind the efficiency with which the chosen tax can be collected.

Every experiment has its value. There is always something to be learned, whether it succeeds or fails. In so far as they succeed, they will create a more peaceful corner or angle, somewhere, in some way, and for a while. Human activity cannot achieve anything more final than that. Even the jubilee has to be repeated again and again. It is important for those who lack adventurous drive themselves to be alert to the experiments going on around them and be receptive to the lessons they provide. Quakers ask themselves, "Are we open to new light, from whatever source it may come?"

In any event there is no point in just waiting for the Peaceable Economy to be delivered ready-made. We must work ceaselessly for it, albeit hoping against hope. In striving to achieve it, we can do no other than follow the exhortation of William the Silent (1533–1584):

One need not hope in order to undertake,
nor succeed in order to persevere.

Afterword:
The Peaceable Kingdom

A shoot will come up from the stump of Jesse; from his roots a Branch will bear fruit.

2 The Spirit of the Lord will rest on him – the Spirit of wisdom and of understanding, the Spirit of counsel and of might, the Spirit of the knowledge and fear of the Lord –

3 and he will delight in the fear of the Lord.

He will not judge by what he sees with his eyes, or decide by what he hears with his ears;

4 but with righteousness he will judge the needy, with justice he will give decisions for the poor of the earth. He will strike the earth with the rod of his mouth; with the breath of his lips he will slay the wicked.

5 Righteousness will be his belt and faithfulness the sash round his waist.

6 The wolf will live with the lamb, the leopard will lie down with the goat,the calf and the lion and the yearling together; and a little child will lead them.

7 The cow will feed with the bear, their young will lie down together, and the lion will eat straw like the ox.

8 The infant will play near the cobra's den, and the young child will put its hand into the viper's nest.

9 They will neither harm nor destroy on all my holy mountain,for the earth will be filled with the knowledge of the Lord as the waters cover the sea. (Is. 11:1-9, NIV)

The painting *The Peaceable Kingdom* by the Pennsylvania Quaker Edward Hicks (1780–1849) is shown on the front cover of this book. He painted the theme over 60 times. The painting illustrates both sides of the passage Isaiah 11:1-9.[1]

The passage in Isaiah begins with a description of the good ruler – indeed the ideal ruler, since the qualities enumerated in verse 2 constitute the basis for the "seven gifts of the Holy Spirit." Isaiah presents the human side of the Peaceable Kingdom as achievable. It is, however, less than perfectly peaceful, since the ruler, ideal though he may be, will still slay the wicked.

In Hicks' painting, the peaceful animals and children of verses 6-9 occupy the foreground. The traditional predator–prey relations have vanished. Even the enmity between humans and snakes, ingrained not only in the Bible but in many popular cultures, has ended. According to Braostoski,[2] for Hicks the animals not only represented their animal selves but also personified traits of human character: rage, egoism, greed, etc. The ox is offering straw to the lion, in a peace-making gesture. According to this interpretation, the second part of the passage from Isaiah concerns the achievement of inner harmony between the warring facets of the human personality.

The cover of this book only shows the right-hand side of the painting. On the left-hand side Hicks represents the social aspect of the Peaceable Kingdom in the background on the left-hand side of the picture. He shows William Penn negotiating with the Indians (as they were then called), certainly a real-world occurrence and widely considered a model of fair dealing. The resulting agreements indeed brought some 70 years of peace between the autochthonous population and the newcomers. Voltaire said it was "the only treaty between these peoples and the Christians which was never sworn to and never broken."[3] The negotiations were essentially economic, concerning land rights and the development of a settler economy: "Although William Penn was granted all the land in Pennsylvania by the King [of England], he and his heirs chose not to grant or settle any part of it without first buying the claims of Indians who lived there."[4]

In the balance between the two parts of his painting, Edward Hicks affirms that the Peaceable Kingdom with its peaceable economy can be achieved in this world.

Abbreviations

ESV   English Standard Version (translation of the Bible)

ILO   International Labour Organization

KJV   King James Version (translation of the Bible)

NIV   New International Version (translation of the Bible)

TOB   Traduction œcuménique de la Bible qv under References.

UNCTAD   United Nations Conference on Trade and Development

UN ESCAP United Nations Economic and Social Commission for Asia and the Pacific.

WIPO   World Intellectual Property Organization

Notes

Chapter 1: Economies and Economics

1. See Setia 2011, p. viii.

2. "Economics," Wikipedia. Regardless of the academic standing of Wikipedia, it reflects a wide slice of informed public opinion. Its definition of economics can therefore be taken as representative.

3. Robbins 1932, p. 15.

4. See Ostrom 1990.

5. Georgescu-Roegen 1971.

6. The leading authority on industrial ecology, which is one approach to this subject, is Suren Erkman. See Erkman 2004, or Erkman & Ramaswamy 2003, which is in English.

7. On the Khian Sea case (1986-1988) see Mitchel Cohen, "Haiti and Toxic Waste," *Counterpunch*, 22-24 January 2010, at: www.counterpunch.org/2010/01/22/haiti-and-toxic-waste/

8. Dommen 1996.

9. Georgescu-Roegen 1971.

10. Calvin, Sermon 137 on Deut. 24:1-6, Biéler p. 361. The quotations from Calvin in this book can generally be found in Biéler 2005. In these cases the reference is given as 'Biéler' followed by the page number. In many cases the translation has been adjusted to fit the present context. Wherever appropriate, epicene language has been used.

11. This succinct statement is supported by Duncan 2012, chap. 4—even though it should be taken as evocative rather than a formal proof.

12. Calvin, Sermon 142 on Deut. 25:1-4, Biéler p. 364.

13. The phrase itself was invented by the British historian Thomas Carlyle (1795–1881).

14. Malthus (1798) 1803, chap. 2.

15. Ibid.

16. Rousseau 1754, part 2.

17. Ibid.

18. Marx 1847.

19. "Great Leap Forward," Wikipedia, at: http://en.wikipedia.org/wiki/Great_Leap_Forward

20. Calvin, Commentary on Psalm 104:15, Biéler p. 204.

21. Gandhi 1960, p. 2.

22. "Economics," investopedia website, at: www.investopedia.com/terms/e/economics.asp

23. *System of National Accounts 2008* 2009.

24. Stiglitz, Sen, & Fitoussi 2009.

25. See for example Rist 2011.

26. See John 18:38.

27. Popper (1934) 1959.

28. Meade 1951a, 1951b. The *Mathematical Supplement* is a delight to the eye because it reproduces the author's actual handwriting where the typesetting techniques of the time couldn't cope with the graphic complexity of the mathematics.

29. Hume, David, 1739, Book 3, Part 1, Section 1.

30. Marshall, Alfred, (1890) 1956, 1. (It might be still better if the word "material" were omitted.).

Chapter 2: Cumulative Causation

1. Myrdal 1957, p. 13.

2. Attributed to Gandhi, see: http://quoteinvestigator.com/2010/12/27/eye-for-eye-blind/

3. The word normally translated by "resist" would be more accurately rendered as "retaliate." Like "talion" in the law of the talion, the word derives from the latin root "talis," "the same as."

4. Note that the parallel with the economy is explicitly brought up here although the passage is primarily concerned with the dynamics of resistance and vengeance.

5. The dictum also appears in Mark 4:25, and Luke 8:18 and 19:26.

6. Woolman 1793, p. 255.

7. All these factors of cumulative causation, and still others, are described in Myrdal 1944 and 1968.

8. The argument that follows rests on Lev. 25 and Deut. 15:1-18 taken together.

9. Woolman 1793, pp. 258-59.

10. Lenin 1917.

11. UNCTAD 1985, esp. pp. 7-13.

12. Marx 1867.

13. Myrdal 1944.

14. Guichonnet 1986.

15. Yari 2004, p. 42.

Chapter. 3: The Economy and the Law

1. Dommen & Faessler 2009, Biéler p. 407

2. Biéler 2005, p. 407

3. James 4.1-2. Cf. p. 28

4. Nestlé, *Code of Business Conduct*, p. 2, at: www.nestle.com/Common/NestleDocuments/Documents/Library/Documents/Corporate_Governance/Code_of_Business_Conduct_EN.pdf

5. Calvin 1845, *Institutes*, 2.7.10. This and all other quotations from this source are translated from the French by author.

6. *Gaudium et spes* 1965, para. 69.1.

7. BP, *Our Commitment to Integrity*, p. 5, at: www.bp.com/liveassets/bp_internet/globalbp/STAGING/global_assets/downloads/C/coc_en_overview.pdf

8. Calvin 1845, *Institutes*, 2.7.12.

Chapter 4: Violence in War and the Economy

1. See, e.g., TOB, Deut. 5:19, and the note to 24:7.

2. Clausewitz 1832-34, book 1, chap. 1.2.

3. Sun Tzu 3.6.

4. Clausewitz 1832-34, book 1, chap. 1.24.

5. In the 1910 translation by Lionel Giles at: www.artofwarsuntzu.com/Art%20of%20War%20PDF.pdf it runs to all of 34 generously spaced pages.

6. Phrase coined by Dwight D. Eisenhower in his farewell address as President of the United States, 17 January 1961.

7. Calvin, Commentary on Exodus 31:2.

8. Clausewitz 1832, book 1, chap. 3.

9. Sun Tzu, 1.18-25.

10. I have not been able to find this much-quoted quotation in *On War*. It has also been attributed to Wellington.

11. Sun Tzu, 11.22.

12. María Soledad Iglesias-Vega, in Harbour & Dommen 2008, p. 209. The order of the two paragraphs has been inverted.

13. Sun Tzu, 3.2.

14. Calvin, Sermon 140 on Deut. 24:14-18, Biéler p. 371.

15. Genesis 1:26 is generally translated as referring to dominion "over all the earth," but the Syriac versions of the text refer to wild animals instead so that the list is exclusively composed of animals.

16. See "Traditional Knowledge," WIPO website, at: http://www.wipo.int/tk/en/

Chapter 5: The Characteristics of Peaceable Economies

1. See TOB, note to Exodus 20:15.

2. Gandhi's Talisman. A free-standing text, 1948. The concept of *swaraj* is explained on p. 85.

3, Beveridge's translation is correct, but at the same time Calvin's phrase has a second, broader, meaning: "what he is in duty bound to provide to them."

4. In French, Calvin uses the word 'charité'. Readers must not let themselves be distracted by the particular sub-meaning generally attached today to 'charity': "giving voluntarily to those in need; alms-giving" (*Concise Oxford Dictionary*). Pope Benedict XVI is in harmony with Calvin when he states that "Love—caritas—is an extraordinary force which leads people to opt for courageous and generous engagement in the field of justice and peace" (Benedict XVI 2009, §1).

5. Calvin's choice of the word 'cupidity' here has a particular point, since it is related to 'covet' (see the *Concise Oxford English Dictionary*).

6. Aquinas, *Summa Contra Gentiles*, 4.55.20.

7. Woolman 1793, chap. 2.

8. Gandhi 1938.

9. Gandhi, M. K., *Young India* 28 June 1928, p. 772.

10. In a letter to Tolstoy.

11. Aristotle, *Politics*, 1.1253a2.

12. Girard (1972) 1977, (1978) 1987.

13. See Calvin box §49.

14. See Calvin box §46

15. Woolman 1793, chap. 3.

16. Claris de Florian 1792. (Le vacher et le garde-chasse.)

17. Ellul 1980.

18. Calvin, Letter to Claude de Sachin.

19. For a development of this theme, see Dommen 1996.

20. World Commission on Environment and Development 1987, p. 43.

21. Which Benjamin Britten incorporated in his *War Requiem* (1962).

22. "About the WTO – A statement by former Director-General Pascal Lamy,"World Trade Organization website, at: http://www.wto.org/english/thewto_e/whatis_e/wto_dg_stat_e.htm consulted on 18.09.2013. Emphasis added.

23. Catechism of the Catholic Church § 2408.

24. Calvin, Sermon 140 on Deut. 24:14-18. Biéler p. 372

25. "Golden Rule," Wikipedia. The article quotes examples from a wide range of cultures.

26. See, for example, Basic Income Earth Network, at: http://www.basicincome.org For a specifically Reformed, if somewhat tongue-in-cheek, presentation, see Dommen 2003.

27. Calvin, Commentary on Mark 10:20. Biéler p. 322

28. Woolman 1793, chap. 1.

29. The phrase has been attributed to, among others, Sarojini Naidu and Mrs. Birla, at whose house Gandhi was living when he was assassinated.

30. Plank 2012, p. 156. The quoted passage is from Woolman.

31. Calvin, Commentary on Matt. 25:27. Biéler 360.

32. Calvin, Commentary on 2 Thess. 3:10. Biéler p. 359.

Chapter 6: Models of Ideal Economy

1. Example from "Is-Ought Problem," Wikipedia.

2. George Fox, *Epistle* 200.

3. Depending on the calendar used.

4. Sahlins 1974.

5. Meade 1989, pp. 1-2.

6. Calvin, Commentary on Gen. 1:26, Biéler p. 204. The "very order of creation" refers of course to the order in which God created things in Gen. 1: everything else was already created by the time he created humanity.

7. Calvin, Commentary on Gen. 2:9, Biéler p. 203.

8. Calvin, Commentary on Gen. 1:15, Biéler p. 353. In Calvin's day, Bible scholars believed that Moses had written its first five books.

9. The French word Calvin uses has both meanings.

10. Calvin, Commentary on Gen. 2:18, Biéler p. 205.

11. The verb "exchange" has a range of meanings; virtually all of them apply here.

12. Calvin, Commentary on Matthew 25:15, 20, Biéler p. 206.

13. Hobbes 1651, chap. 13.

14. Hume 1739, book 3, part 2, sect. 2.

15. Ibid.

16. Letter from Voltaire to Rousseau, 30 August 1755.

17. Rousseau 1754. The quotations are translated by ED.

18. Arcidiacono, 2011, note 182, p. 258.

19. Ibid., part 2.

20. Defoe 1719.

21. Ibid., p. 244.

22. Mottu 2011, p. 120.

23. For example, The English Standard Version, the Common English Bible, or The New American Standard Bible. See the comment in *Le Nouveau Testament commenté*.

24. Calvin 1845, 4.1.3.

25. Ragaz 1942, 7th dialogue.

Chapter 7: Can We Get There from Here?

1. Smith 1776, book 4, chap. 2.

2. Calvin, Letter to Claude de Sachin.

3. "Award Ceremony Speech," Nobelprize.org, 10 December 2010, at: http://www.nobelprize.org/nobel_prizes/economics/laureates/2010/presentation-speech.html. The laureates were Peter A. Diamond, Dale T. Mortensen, and Christopher A. Pissarides.

4. Regarding Müntzer, see e.g., Brendler 1989.

5. See e.g., *The New York Times*, 26 November 2006.

6. Personal communication.

7. Sen 1977, p. 317.

8. Miguel d'Escoto Brockmann, President of the 63rd session of the United Nations General Assembly, in the Foreword to United Nations, 2009.

9. The italics are in the original.

Chapter 8: Alternatives to Violence

1. Calvin 1545, p. 220.

2. Schumacher 1973.

3. See Walvin 1997 as one example among many studies of this kind of trend.

4. Taken from the cover of Töpffer 1835.

5. As of 10 October 2012.

6. This passage is translated from Höffe 1983 by ED. Note that the phrase *Human, all too human* is the title of a work by Friedrich Nietzsche (1878).

7. Santayana 1905-1906, vol. 1.

8. Matthew 18:12-14.

9. A paraphrase of the first sentence of the defintion of "sustainable development" in World Commission on Environment and Development 1987, p. 43.

10. "Buyers and sellers" includes workers and employers.

11. This does not necessarily mean compensating them: see Dommen 1993, p. 17.

Afterword: The Peaceable Kingdom

1. For an authoritative commentary on the painting, see Braostoski 2000.

2. Ibid.

3. "Quakers," in Voltaire 1764. Quakers refuse to swear.
4. "Pennsylvania on the Eve of Colonization," Pennsylvania History, website of the State of Pennsylvania, at: http://www.legis.state.pa.us/wu01/vc/visitor_info/pa_history/pa_history.htm

Bibliography

Aquinas, Thomas, *Summa Contra Gentiles*

Arcidiacono, Bruno, 2011, *Cinq types de paix: une histoire des plans de pacification perpétuelle (XVIIᵉ - XXᵉ siècle)*, Paris, Presses universitaires de France.

Aristotle, *The Politics*. There are many editions and translations. One attractive one available online is Benjamin Jowett's (Oxford 1885), http://files.libertyfund.org/files/819/0033-02_Bk_SM.pdf

Benedict XVI, 2009, Encyclical letter *Caritas in Veritate*.

Biéler, André, 2005, *Calvin's Economic and Social Thought*, ed. Edward Dommen, Geneva, World Alliance of Reformed Churches and World Council of Churches.

Braostoski, John, 2000, "Hicks's Peaceable Kingdom," *Friends Journal*, February, at: http://www2.gol.com/users/quakers/Hicks_Peaceable_Kingdom.htm

Brendler, Gerhard, 1989, *Thomas Müntzer*, Berlin, VEB Deutscher Verlag der Wissenschaften.

Calvin, John, 1845, *Institutes of the Christian Religion*, trans. Edward Dommen, from the French, based on trans. Henry

Beveridge from the Latin (1845). Extracts taken from http://www.ccel.org/ccel/calvin/institutes

———, 1545, *Against the Fanatical and Furious Sect of the Libertines*, in Opera Calvini Vol. VII

Catechism of the Catholic Church, available online at http://www.vatican.va/archive/ENG0015/__P8B.HTM

Claris de Florian, Jean-Pierre, 1792, *Fables*.

Clausewitz, Carl von, 1832-34, *Vom Kriege* (On war). There are numerous translations. Those available online are old; the more recent ones, still under copyright, may be more reliable or at least more in line with present-day conceptions.

Concise Oxford Dictionary, 1995, 9th ed., unless otherwise specified.

Defoe, Daniel, 1719, *The Life and Strange Surprizing Adventures of Robinson Crusoe*, at: http://www.pierre-marteau.com/editions/1719-robinson-crusoe.html

Dommen, Edward, 1993, Fair Principles for Sustainable Development, Aldershot, Edward Elgar.

———, 1996, "La colonisation de l'avenir: deux exemples énergétiques," in *Le droit international face à l'éthique et à la politique de l'environnement*, Ivo Rens et Joel Jakubec, Geneva, SEBES.

———, 1999, "Heureux anniversaire Sisyphe ! Une analyse économique du mythe du Jubilé," in *Debt and the Jubilee, Pacing the Economy*, ed. Jean-Michel Bonvin, Geneva, Observatoire de la Finance.

————, 2003a, *How Just is the Market Economy?*, Geneva, World Council of Churches Publications.

————, 2003b, "Si tout est donné, pourquoi travailler?" in *Un revenu de base pour chacun(e)*, Andràs November et Guy Standing, Geneva, International Labour Office, at: http://www.basicincome.org/bien/pdf/2002Dommen.pdf

Dommen, Edouard, and Marc Faessler, 2009, "Calvin et le prêt à intérêt," in *Pratiques financières, regards chrétiens*, Paul Dembinski, Paris, Desclée de Brouwer.

Duncan, Richard, 2012, *The New Depression: The Breakdown of the Paper Money Economy*, John Wiley & Sons.

Ellul, Jacques, 1980, *La foi au prix du doute*, Paris, Hachette.

Encyclopédie du protestantisme, 1995, Geneva, éditions Labor et Fides.

Erkman, Suren, 2004, *Vers une écologie industrielle*, Paris, éditions Charles Léopold Mayer, 2nd ed., at: http://docs.eclm.fr/pdf_livre/285.pdf

Erkman, Suren, and Ramesh Ramaswamy, 2003, *Applied Industrial Ecology.: A New Platform for Planning Sustainable Societies. Focus on Developing Countries with Case Studies from India*, Bangalore, Aicra Publishers.

Fox, George, *Epistles,* at: http://esr.earlham.edu/qbi/gfe/e200-206.htm.

Gandhi, M. K., 1938, *Hind Swaraj or Indian Home Rule*, Ahmedabad, Navajivan Publishing House.

————, 1960, *Trusteeship*, compiled by Ravindra Kelkar, Navaji-van Mudranalaya, Ahmedabad, at: www.mkgandhi.org/ebks/trusteeship.pdf

Gaudium et spes, 1965, Pastoral Constitution adopted by the Council Vatican II, at: http://www.vatican.va/archive/hist_councils/ii_vatican_council/documents/vat-ii_const_19651207_gaudium-et-spes_en.html

Georgescu-Roegen, Nicholas, 1971, *The Entropy Law and the Economic Process*, Cambridge, Harvard University Press.

Girard, René, (1972) 1977, *Violence and the Sacred*, trans. Patrick Gregory, Baltimore, Johns Hopkins University Press.

————, (1978) 1987, *Things Hidden since the Foundation of the World*, Stanford, Stanford University Press.

Guichonnet, Paul, ed., 1986, *Histoire de Genève*, Toulouse, Privat, 3rd. ed.

Harbour, Randall, and Edouard Dommen, 2008, *Les liaisons fructueuses*, Geneva, Geneva International Academic Network.

Hobbes, 1651, *Leviathan*, at: http://oregonstate.edu/instruct/phl302/texts/hobbes/leviathan-contents.html

Höffe, Otfried, (1976) 1983, *Dictionnaire de Morale*, édition française adaptée et augmentée sous la direction de Philibert Secrétan, Fribourg, éditions universitaires.

Hume, David, 1739, *A Treatise of Human Nature*, at: http://oll.libertyfund.org/index.php?option=com_staticxt&staticfile=show.php%3Ftitle=342&Itemid=27

Lenin, Vladimir Ilyich, 1917, *Imperialism, the Highest Stage of Capitalism,* at: http://www.marxists.org/archive/lenin/works/pdf/Lenin_Imperialism_the_Highest_Stahe_of_Capitalism.pdf

Malthus, Thomas Robert, (1798) 1803, *Essay on the Principle of Population* (2d ed.).

Marshall, Alfred, (1890) 1956, *Principles of Economics*, London, Macmillan, 8th ed.

Marx, Karl, 1847, *Wages,* quoted in the Wikipedia article, "Reserve army of labour."

Marx, Karl, 1867, *Capital,* (English trans. 1887), at: http://libcom.org/library/capital-karl-marx

Mauss, Marcel, 1923-1924, "Essai sur le don : Forme et raison de l'échange dans les sociétés archaïques," *Année sociologique*, seconde série (trans. W. D. Halls, 2002, *The Gift: The Form and Reason for Exchange in Archaic Societies*, Routledge) at: http://anthropomada.com/bibliotheque/Marcel-MAUSS-Essai-sur-le-don.pdf.

Meade, James Edward, 1951a, *The Balance of Payments*, Oxford University Press.

———, 1951b, *The Balance of Payments, Mathematical Supplement,* Oxford University Press.

———, 1989, *Agathotopia: The Economics of Partnership*, Aberdeen University Press.

Mottu, Henry, 2011, *Recommencer l'Église*, Geneva, Labor et Fides.

Myrdal, Gunnar, 1944, *An American Dilemma: the Negro Problem and Modern Democracy*, New York, Harper.

———, 1957, *Economic Theory and Under-Developed Regions*, London, Duckworth.

———, 1968, *Asian Drama, An Enquiry into the Poverty of Nations*, New York, Pantheon.

Nouveau Testament commenté, 2012, sous la direction de Camille Focant et Daniel Marguerat, Paris, Bayard; Genève, Labor et Fides.

Ostrom, Elinor, 1990, *Governing the Commons: The Evolution of Institutions for Collective Action*, Cambridge University Press.

Plank, Geoffrey, 2012, *John Woolman's Path to the Peaceable Kingdom*, University of Pennsylvania Press.

Popper, Karl R., (1934) 1959, *The Logic of Scientific Discovery*, London, Hutchinson & Co.

Ragaz, Leonhard, 1942, *Die Botschaft vom Reiche Gottes. Ein Katechismus für Erwachsene*, Bern, Herbert Lang.

Rist, Gilbert, 2011, *The Delusions of Economics: The Misguided Certainties of a Hazardous Science*, London, Zed Books.

Robbins, Lionel, 1932, *An Essay on the Nature and Significance of Economic Science,* London, Macmillan.

Rousseau, Jean-Jacques, 1754, *Discourse on the origin of inequality among men*, trans. G.D.H. Cole.

Sahlins, Marshall David, 1974 (1972?), *Stone Age Economics*, Transaction Publishers, New Jersey.

Santayana, George, 1905-1906, *The Life of Reason*, at: http://www.gutenberg.org/files/15000/15000-h/15000-h.htm

Schumacher, Ernst Friedrich, 1973, *Small Is Beautiful: Economics As If People Mattered,* Harper & Row.

Sen, Amartya K., 1977, "Rational Fools: A Critique of the Behavioural Foundations of Economic Theory," *Philosophy and Public Affairs* 6/4: 317-44.

Setia, Adi, 2011, *The Book of Earning a Livelihood*, Al-Imam Muhammad Ibn Al-Hasan Al-Shaybani, trans. with.intro. and notes by Adi Setia, Kuala Lumpur, IBFIM.

Smith, Adam, 1776, *The Wealth of Nations.* Several online editions are available.

Stiglitz, Joseph E., Amartya Sen and Jean-Paul Fitoussi, 2009, *Report by the Commission on the Measurement of Economic Performance and Social Progress*, at: www.stiglitz-sen-fitoussi.fr

Sun Tzu, *The Art of War*, at: http://classics.mit.edu/Tzu/artwar.html

System of National Accounts 2008, 2009, New York (EC, IMF, OECD, UN, and the World Bank), at: http://unstats.un.org/unsd/nationalaccount/docs/SNA2008.pdf

TOB *Traduction œcuménique de la Bible*, 2010, Paris, éditions du Cerf.

Töpffer, Rodolphe, 1983, *Du progrès dans ses rapports avec le petit bourgeois* (1835), Cognac, éditions Le temps qu'il fait.

UNCTAD, 1985, *The History of UNCTAD 1964-1984*, New York, United Nations, UNCTAD/OSG/286.

UN ESCAP 2004, *Bulletin on Asia-Pacific Perspectives 2003/04.*

United Nations, 2009, *Report of the Commission of Experts of the President of the United Nations General Assembly on Reforms of the International Monetary and Financial System*, 21 September.

Voltaire, 1764, *Dictionnaire philosophique*. Several versions are available online.

Walvin, James, 1997, *The Quakers: Money & Morals*, London, John Murray.

Woolman, John, 1793, *A Plea for the Poor*, in *The Journal and Major Essays of John Woolman*, ed. Moulton, Phillips P., New York, Oxford University Press, 1971. Also at: http://www.umilta.net/woolmanplea.html

World Commission on Environment and Development, 1987, *Our Common Future*, Oxford University Press.

Yari, Marin, 2004, *Beyond "Subsistence Affluence": Poverty in Pacific Island Countries* chap. 3 in UN ESCAP at: http://www.unescap.org/pdd/publications/bulletin03-04/bulletin03-04_ch3.pdf